The Motivation to Vote

The Motivation to Vote

Explaining Electoral Participation

ANDRÉ BLAIS
AND
JEAN-FRANÇOIS DAOUST

UBCPress · Vancouver · Toronto

30 29 28 27 26 25 24 23 22 21 20   5 4 3 2 1

Printed in Canada on FSC-certified ancient-forest-free paper
(100% post-consumer recycled) that is processed chlorine- and acid-free.

Library and Archives Canada Cataloguing in Publication

Title: The motivation to vote: explaining electoral participation /
André Blais and Jean-François Daoust.
Names: Blais, André, 1947 – author. | Daoust, Jean-François, 1992 – author.
Description: Includes bibliographical references and index.
Identifiers: Canadiana (print) 20190223235 | Canadiana (ebook) 20190223332 |
ISBN 9780774862677 (hardcover) | ISBN 9780774862691 (PDF) |
ISBN 9780774862707 (EPUB) | ISBN 9780774862714 (Kindle)
Subjects: LCSH: Elections. | LCSH: Voting. | LCSH: Voting research. |
LCSH: Political participation.
Classification: LCC JF1001.B53 2020 | DDC 324.6–dc23

Canadä

UBC Press gratefully acknowledges the financial support for our publishing
program of the Government of Canada (through the Canada Book Fund),
the Canada Council for the Arts, and the British Columbia Arts Council.

This book has been published with the help of a grant from the
Canadian Federation for the Humanities and Social Sciences, through the
Awards to Scholarly Publications Program, using funds provided
by the Social Sciences and Humanities Research Council of Canada.

Printed and bound in Canada by Friesens
Set in Univers Condensed and Minion by Artegraphica Design Co. Ltd.
Copy editor: Frank Chow
Indexer: Judy Dunlop

UBC Press
The University of British Columbia
2029 West Mall
Vancouver, BC V6T 1Z2
www.ubcpress.ca

Contents

Figures and Tables

Figures

Tables

Acknowledgments

We benefited from many insights from numerous scholars, colleagues, and friends while working on this project. Notably, we had the opportunity to present some of our findings at the weekly joint seminar of the Canada Research Chair in Electoral Democracy and the Research Chair in Electoral Studies at the Université de Montréal, the Political Behaviour Seminar at London School of Economics (LSE), and the Working Group in Political Psychology and Behaviour (WoGPop) at Harvard University. We thank participants in these seminars, and especially Elisabeth Gidengil, Carol Galais, Damien Bol, Aina Gallego, Filip Kostelka, and Mathieu Turgeon for comments on earlier drafts of the manuscript.

We are also thankful to Kelly Blidook, who suggested that we meet with UBC Press, and we thank the UBC Press team for their collaboration.

This book is largely based on data collected through the Making Electoral Democracy Work (MEDW) project. We thank the Social Sciences and Humanities Research Council of Canada for its financial support and all those involved in the project for their collaboration.

The Motivation to Vote

1

The Decision to Vote or Not to Vote

Life is about making decisions, many small and a few big ones. Some decisions are made every day (what time should I get up?), others are made only once (or a few times) in a lifetime (what name should I give to my child?). Some decisions are made after a long process of reflection or deliberation (should I buy a house?) while others are made on the go, on the inspiration of the moment or gut feelings (should I have another beer?). Some are very personal (what should I eat at the cafeteria today?) and others are made jointly with others (what should we have for our Christmas dinner?).

The decision to vote or not to vote in an election can be deemed to be trivial. It is a small decision that we make rather infrequently and that has little or no consequence, for us as well as for society. The probability that a single vote will decide the outcome of an election is close to nil (Downs 1957; Mueller 2003; Owen and Grofman 1984), and so whether or not one votes will not decide which party will win the election.

Yet the decision to vote or abstain is not so inconsequential. First, it is not as infrequent as it may seem. In this century, that is, in the last nineteen years, the senior co-author of this book had to make that decision in seven (Canadian) federal elections, five (Quebec) provincial elections, and six (Montreal) local elections – once a year on average. This is in a country where there is no presidential or second chamber election. In many places, there are also referenda, where the same decision to vote or not to vote needs to be made. The average citizen living in a democratic country where she acquires the right to vote at age eighteen and has a life expectancy of seventy-five years has the opportunity to vote in an election or referendum more than fifty times in her lifetime.

Whether we choose to vote or abstain tells us (and others) a lot about *who* we are. As we show later, the decision to vote or not to vote very much reflects what we like and do not like, in life and in society, and our values, particularly our conception of citizens' rights and duties in the polity. It is a decision that is affected not only by our self-identity, our feelings, and our beliefs but also by concrete cost-benefit instrumental considerations. It is both personal and social. It is affected by ethical views, even though our choices are not always consistent with our ethical aspirations. In short, it is a quintessential human decision, based on a combination of emotions and instrumental calculations, full of complexities, ambiguities, and sometimes contradictions.

Furthermore, the decision that most of us make most of the time, that is, to vote rather than to abstain, is paradoxical, in the sense that the rational person who calculates the personal benefits and costs of voting should come to the conclusion that she should abstain. She should abstain because the expected personal benefit of voting is extraordinarily tiny since the probability that her vote will decide the outcome is close to nil. Whether or not she votes will not decide who will be elected president or which party(ies) will form the government. Therefore, whenever there is some cost in voting, whether it is the time that it takes to go to the polling station and vote and/or the time to become informed in order to decide which party/candidate to support, the rational person should abstain (Downs 1957).

Yet turnout in national elections is typically around 70% (Blais 2018, using IDEA data), and so most citizens appear to make an "irrational" decision. This is known as the voting paradox. Our aim in this book is *not* to evaluate the merits and limits of rational choice theory (see Blais 2000). But the fact that most people appear to be "irrational," that there is this apparent "paradox of voting," highlights the relevance of the question. There is no obvious answer to the question of why people vote. This is an enigma.

For all these reasons (and we suppose many others that we are unaware of), we decided to devote a good fraction of our time to addressing the turnout puzzle. We reveal how, after doing much research of our own, reading, discussing, and reflecting on the rich literature on the topic and related issues, we make sense of the simple act of voting or not voting. We present empirical evidence that supports our model. We argue that the decision to vote or abstain hinges on two basic predispositions (interest in politics and civic duty) and two election-specific judgments (caring and ease of voting). Clearly this is not an exhaustive model; many other attitudes come into play. Our claim is that with these four factors we can understand the basic motivations behind the turnout decision.

We focus on the individual-level determinants of turnout, that is, on the attitudes and judgments that lead someone to vote or abstain. There is a rich literature on the contextual factors that contribute to a higher or lower turnout (for a review and meta-analysis, see Blais 2006; Geys 2006; Cancela and Geys 2016; Stockemer 2017). Turnout, for instance, is higher when it is a close contest, when the office to be filled is more powerful, and when the previous election is not too recent (Blais and Dobrzynska 1998; Franklin 2004; Kostelka 2015). We do not deny the importance of these contextual factors (though many of the findings, especially with respect to the effect of the electoral system, do not seem very robust; see Blais 2006; Blais and Aarts 2006) but we wish to concentrate on the individual-level factors in this study.

It is possible that individual-level determinants of turnout vary across contexts (see Kittilson and Anderson 2011). We have no doubt that this is at least partly the case. For instance, the relationship between interest and politics is unlikely to be exactly the same in every country and in every type of election. Yet we start with the assumption that the motivations for voting and abstaining are basically the same in all elections, and that the impact of contextual factors is mostly additive – that is, on top and independent of the individual-level factors. We revisit this assumption in Chapter 8.

The Framework

We construe the decision to vote or abstain as hinging upon the answers that each individual gives to four questions: (1) Do I like politics? (2) Do I have a duty to vote? (3) Do I care about the outcome? and (4) Do I find it easy to vote?

In the beginning, a person is either interested in politics or not. There are those who like politics and those who don't, just as there are some who do or do not like sports, arts, or religion. There are many reasons why people are more interested in some domains than in others. Our goal is not to understand why some people are interested in politics whereas others are not, though this would be a fascinating (and complex) study. Rather, we take this as a given, and look instead at how political interest, which we take to be equivalent to liking politics, affects the propensity to vote.

The basic intuition is simple and straightforward. If someone finds tennis exciting, she is prone to want to play and watch tennis and keep up with many events related to that sport. If someone finds it boring, then she sees little reason to follow it. The same rationale applies to politics – that is, some of us find it exciting and follow it passionately while others find it boring, complicated, or threatening, and they do not care about it or may even try to avoid it as much as possible (Hibbing and Theiss-Morse 2002).

These differences in taste are profound and enduring. Markus Prior (2010, 757), who has examined the stability of political interest over the life cycle with long-term panel data, arrives at the following conclusion: "Of the 58 stability coefficients ... for panel waves that occurred one year apart, only 10 have 95% intervals that do *not* include 1.0." Therefore, "people return to their stable long-term political interest levels quickly after perturbations caused by political or personal events. In short, political interest behaves like a central element of *political identity*, not like a frequently updated attitude" (763, emphasis added).

Being interested or not in politics is not a simple matter of taste; it defines who we are.

It is not farfetched to predict that those who are interested in politics are likely to vote and those who have no interest are inclined to abstain. There are of course other factors at play, but one's level of interest in politics, which remains remarkably stable over time, acts as a strong predisposition. Those who like politics like elections, and those who dislike politics dislike elections. The relationship is not perfect, as it is possible to be very interested in politics and to have little concern for a specific election, but we expect most of those who are interested in politics to find most elections exciting and to want to participate most of the time. The opposite should hold for those with little or no interest in politics.

This assumes that the driving force behind the decision to vote or abstain is *motivation* (hence the title of this book). The main reason, therefore, why many people do not vote is simply that they have little incentive to vote – they are not psychologically engaged. Contrary to Henry Brady and colleagues (1995), who argue that the main reason for lack of political participation is lack of resources, we assume that the main reason why some people do not participate in elections is that they do not want to – that is, motivation matters more than resources. The resource model is certainly relevant to the study of political participation broadly defined, but it is much less useful with respect to electoral participation, as Brady and colleagues (1995, 283) themselves acknowledge: "Indeed, political interest is much more important than resources if our main project is to explain voting turnout." Thus, the first question we should ask someone if we want to understand why she decided to vote or not is simply whether she likes politics.

The extent to which someone is interested in politics is not the only predisposition that matters. Quite a few people want to vote even though they are not interested in politics. The reason is their belief that they ought to vote, no matter how they feel about politics, elections, parties, or candidates. They believe that they have a moral obligation to vote, that is, they have a civic duty to participate in an election.

In a democracy, every citizen over a certain age has the right to vote. Whether citizens have a duty to vote is ambiguous. In countries where voting is compulsory, citizens have a legal duty to vote. Our study focuses on countries where voting is voluntary, but we should keep in mind that voting is officially defined as a legal duty to participate in many democracies (Singh 2019).

In those countries where voting is formally voluntary, the public discourse is ambiguous. While it is recognized that people have the right to abstain, there is the public norm that the *good* citizen has a civic duty to vote (provided it is not too complicated to do so; being sick, for instance, is a completely acceptable reason for abstaining). When asked in 1944 whether they see voting "more as a duty you owe to your country or more as a right to use if you want to," 59% of Americans chose "a duty" and 36% "a right" (Dennis 1970, 827). More recently, when asked how important it is for the good citizen to always vote in elections on a scale from 1 to 7, the mean score was 6.2, just slightly lower than the score for obeying the laws (Dalton 2008, 30). Moreover, about 90% of Canadians and 80% of British citizens agree with the statement that "it is the duty of every citizen to vote" (Blais 2000, 95).

The reasons why many people believe that they have a duty to vote are not always clear. One way to think about this is that people are motivated by reciprocity (Falk and Fischbacher 2006). The basic idea is that people wish to reward kind actions and punish bad ones. There is a huge experimental literature that supports the theory (see Dufwenberg and Kirsteiger 2004; Cox 2004). In the case at hand, when people are given a right that they cherish (the right to vote), they feel that they should reciprocate, and the most obvious way to reciprocate is to make use of that right. Another interpretation is that the civic norm of duty is learned at the community level. David Campbell (2006), especially, shows that the school and community civic climate at the time of adolescence affects adults' willingness to be politically active years later.

Whatever the reasons underlying the belief that there is a civic duty to vote, there is little doubt that many people subscribe to this view.

At the same time, we should not overstate support for this norm. It is politically correct to say that there is a civic duty to vote. We assume that indeed quite a few people strongly adhere to the view that they have a moral obligation to vote and that this strongly affects their decision to vote. But there are also many people who adhere to the opposite norm, that people are free to do what they want in a democracy and that there is nothing wrong with deciding not to vote. There are also many who do not have clear views either way, who pay lip service to the public norm when responding to a survey but who have not truly internalized the norm that citizens have a duty to vote in elections. The challenge is to sort out those who truly believe that they have a duty to vote.

It is useful to point out the similarities and differences in how political interest and sense of duty influence the decision to vote. Both are strong *predispositions* that people develop early in life and that are mostly stable over time. We have referred earlier to Prior's work (2010) demonstrating the remarkable stability of political interest. We do not have similar long-term panel data for sense of duty, but the evidence that we do have suggests strong stability. André Blais and Chris Achen (2019) report strong correlations over four waves, covering one year, during the 2008 American presidential election. Carol Galais and André Blais (2016a) find similarly strong over-time correlations in Spain over a period of eighteen months (four waves).

What is also common to political interest and sense of civic duty is that both are *general* predispositions that lead people to vote or abstain in any election. The other two considerations that we discuss below are more election-specific and vary over time, depending on the specificities of the context. Interest and duty act as broad attitudes that push individuals in one direction (voting or abstaining) in the absence of countervailing factors.

What distinguishes duty from political interest is that it is *moral*. The person who is interested in politics is inclined to vote because she *wants* to. The person who believes there is a civic duty to vote is inclined to go to the polling station because she feels she *ought* to. The interested person enjoys voting because politics is exciting. The dutiful citizen decides to vote because her conscience tells her that she must do it; it is a duty that, like many other duties, needs to be fulfilled because it is the right thing to do. Duty therefore motivates one to vote in a different way than interest. The driving mechanism is normative rather than affective.

We expect those who are interested in politics to have a stronger sense of duty. After all, those who like politics have a positive prejudice about political matters, and they should be prone to think that people should participate in politics in general and particularly in elections. The relationship should be far from perfect, however. Some people are generally prone to think in terms of obligations, whereas others are deeply suspicious of so-called duties. People have different conceptions of what citizenship does and does not entail, and these conceptions are bound to shape their views about whether they have an ethical obligation to vote or whether it is a matter of personal choice.

The last two considerations that come into play in the turnout decision are at least partly election-specific. The first is how much the individual cares about the outcome. This "how much does it matter?" question corresponds to the B term in the rational calculus of voting model (Downs 1957; Riker and Ordeshook 1968). It boils down to whether, and how much, the person prefers one of the parties.[1]

As elegantly explicated by Anthony Downs (1957), in a two-party system, the citizen seeks to determine what each party will do over the course of the next mandate if it wins the election. If she believes that the two parties will adopt the same policies, she is indifferent and has no reason to vote. She is also indifferent if she expects the two parties to implement different policies but these policies are equally satisfactory or unsatisfactory, or if these differences concern issues that she does not care about. In short, the citizen votes only if she feels that the parties differ in meaningful ways about the issues that she is personally concerned with.

From this perspective, two conditions must be met for a person to care about the outcome of the election. First, she must care about the main issues that are debated in the campaign. Second, she must believe that the decisions that will be made about these issues depend to a good extent on who will be elected. If either of these conditions is absent, the person is indifferent, and she has no reason to vote. It should be pointed out, however, that it is possible for a citizen to care a lot about the outcome of an election without paying much attention to the issues. This would be the case of voters who strongly prefer a given party, for example, because they trust its leader or simply because they identify with the party and are thus convinced that it is the best to govern the polity.

We expect this third consideration of our model, that is, "caring," to be positively correlated with political interest for three reasons. The first is that those who like and follow politics are more likely to be aware of differences between the parties. Those who do not follow politics regularly may be only vaguely aware of the positions of the parties and are unlikely to devote much effort to finding out these positions. The second reason is that those interested in politics are more prone to developing strong views and preferences, and thus to care a lot about what the government should and should not do. Again, the uninterested are more likely to care about who will win the football championship or who will win the Grammy Awards. The third reason is that the uninterested are more likely to distrust everything that politicians say during an election campaign. When you do not like politics, you are likely to dislike politicians and to be skeptical of their promises. The consequence is that the parties and candidates may all look alike.

The relationship between lack of general political interest and indifference in a specific election should be only moderately strong, however. Even the uninterested sometime get excited in a specific election and/or about a special issue, or they are attracted to a specific party or leader. Conversely, those who follow politics regularly may occasionally find little meaningful differences between the parties or they may not care about the issues discussed in a campaign. The relationship between duty and caring should be even weaker, especially once we take into account individuals' level of political interest. There should be some relationship since those who believe that they have a moral obligation to vote may also think that they have a moral obligation to cast an informed vote (see Blais, Galais, and Mayer 2019), and so are more likely to search for at least some information about the parties. This should facilitate the process of forming an opinion about what the "good" and the "bad" options are. The dutiful person, however, does not have the inner motivation to follow politics closely (unless she is already very interested) and so is bound to pay little attention to an election campaign, and her preferences will often be relatively weak.

The fourth and last factor in our model is the perceived ease/difficulty of voting. This is the cost term ("C") in the rational calculus of voting. We start with the assumption that for most people most of the time voting is easy, and this explains in part why turnout is relatively high. It is precisely because voting is a simple, undemanding act that so many people believe they have a moral duty to vote. Most people would find it unreasonable to require all citizens to participate actively in groups, organizations, parties, or demonstrations, but should not the "good" citizen do her part and contribute a little bit of her time and go to the polling station?

Going to the polling station is easy for most people, but it is difficult or complicated for some.[2] It is not easy for all those who happen to be sick or away from home on the day of the election. It may not be easy for all those who suffer from some handicap. For some it may be a source of stress. In that case, going to the polling station as such is easy, but they may not know or understand exactly what they are supposed to do, what the ballot paper looks like, and what they are supposed to write on that ballot. Even in our advanced societies there are many people who are practically illiterate; for many of them, the act of voting is far from simple. In those circumstances, staying home has a lot of appeal.

Since Downs (1957), researchers distinguish between the cost of going to the polling station and the cost of looking for information to help one make up one's mind which party to vote for. This distinction is not as straightforward as it may first appear. The cost of finding information about the parties is clearly higher for those who do not like politics and do not follow the news, but the crux of the problem is that such people lack the motivation to follow politics to begin with;

they are not interested in politics. Similarly, those who have formed strong preferences about the issues and the parties face little information cost, but this is simply because they care a lot about the outcome of the election.

In this study, we do not distinguish between voting and information costs (but see Blais et al. 2019). We simply rely on people's overall subjective judgment about how easy or complicated they find voting to be. Because it is a subjective perception, it is likely to be shaped in part by people's predispositions, most strongly their interest in politics and secondarily their sense of civic duty, as well as by how much they care about the outcome. Still, these correlations should not be very strong, since most of us sometimes find ourselves in situations where we are sick, depressed, or overwhelmed with more pressing concerns. And it is fair to predict that whenever the cost of voting becomes high, the temptation to stay home becomes strong.

Our main goal is to show that these four basic factors (interest, duty, caring, and ease) help us a lot in making sense of the decision to vote or abstain. The first three are clearly motivational factors and are thus perfectly in line with our motivational account of the turnout decision. Ease of voting needs to be incorporated as an additional factor, but it is clearly as individual and subjective as the first three factors.

We then devote an entire chapter to an alternative explanation of turnout that has gained popularity in the recent literature, namely, that voting is a habit (see especially Franklin 2004). This interpretation is based on the accurate observation that the decisions that people make to vote or abstain in different elections are not independent. A person who voted (or abstained) in the previous election is likely to vote (or abstain) in the next one. From this observation, it is a small step to inferring that voting is a habit that people display repeatedly over time.

We do not dismiss the possibility that voting is a habit for some people, but it is strange to have a habit involving something that occurs relatively infrequently and irregularly. We pointed out earlier that people typically decide whether or not to vote about once a year. This is not frequent enough to develop a habit, we believe, especially since the timing is irregular, and the rules and the set of options (the parties) often vary across types of elections.

Furthermore, and most importantly, people may well repeat the same behaviour over time simply because the values and/or attitudes that drive their behaviour remain the same. Someone who is very interested in politics or has a strong sense of duty is prone to vote in every election, especially as interest and duty are unlikely to vary substantially over time. The opposite holds if the person is uninterested in politics and does not believe that she has a moral obligation to vote. As Eric Plutzer (2002) notes, it is important to distinguish between persistence and inertia (habit). We should point to the presence of habit only if we can show that the turnout decision in an election depends on the turnout decision made in the previous election, not on the factors that shaped the initial decision. We perform more appropriate tests of the habit hypothesis, and find little support for it.

Finally, we consider contextual effects. Traditionally, there have been two separate streams of research on turnout (Blais 2006). One stream is based on aggregate turnout data and focuses on the contextual-level factors (mostly institutional) that are associated with lower or higher participation rates. The second is based on survey data and examines the individual-level factors (mostly attitudinal) that are associated with the propensity to vote. More recently, an important new stream of research has attempted to combine these two approaches. With the advent of large datasets combining survey data from many different elections and countries, through such initiatives such as the Comparative Study of Electoral Systems (CSES), it has become possible to estimate within the same model the effect of both individual and contextual factors. In this context, special emphasis has been placed on discovering *interaction* effects, whereby the impact of individual variables is *conditional* on contextual factors (see Anderson and Dalton 2011).

We see a lot of merit in this new approach. The Making Electoral Democracy Work (MEDW) data that we use in this study are precisely based on the idea that it is crucial to look at how the rules of the game (the institutions) affect not only parties' and voters' behaviour but also *how* they make up their minds – that is, the considerations that shape their decisions.

Yet we claim that the considerations that lead people to vote or not to vote are basically the same in all elections. We therefore start with a simple model that is tested with a merged dataset that includes all the elections covered by MEDW data. In the last chapter, we explicitly test for interaction effects between the four individual-level attitudes and contextual variables. We do find some context-specific patterns, but we show that they are relatively rare and that their impact is, in substantial terms, modest. We conclude that it is fair to assert that in established democracies people decide to vote or not to vote for similar reasons across all kinds of contexts.

The Approach

For most of the analyses, we use the MEDW surveys that were conducted in five countries between 2011 and 2015 (Blais 2010a; Stephenson et al. 2017): Canada, France, Spain, Switzerland, and Germany. These countries were chosen mainly because, although all are by now established and developed democracies, they differ most especially with respect to electoral system. Canada and France both have "majoritarian" rules for their national elections, Canada a first-past-the-post system and France a two-round system; Spain and Switzerland have proportional representation, while Germany has a compensatory mixed voting system.

We do not claim that these countries constitute a representative sample of established democracies. Europe is overrepresented, but clearly Europe dominates the list of established democracies, especially those with voluntary voting. There is an overrepresentation of federal and relatively decentralized countries, as well as of countries with supranational elections (mostly due to the overrepresentation of Europe). These biases should be kept in mind.

What is more important is that these countries represent a great variety of contexts. Some countries (France and Germany) are quite large in terms of population, and one (Switzerland) is very small. At the time of our study, two countries (France and Spain) were in deep recession while the economic situation in the other three countries was relatively good. As mentioned above, these countries have very different voting systems. By combining these diversified cases, we hope to highlight the common patterns that emerge when it comes to deciding whether to vote or not. At the same time, it should be clear that our interpretation is confined to established democracies where voting is not compulsory. How the model would need to be modified in the case of non-established democracies (or non-democratic elections) and/or when voting is made compulsory is explored in the conclusion.

Turnout in the five countries considered here is somewhat lower than the average in contemporary democracies for national lower house elections, which is about 70% of registered electors (Blais 2018). Turnout in the MEDW national lower house elections was 49% in Switzerland (2011), 55% in France (2012), 69% in Canada (2015) and Spain (2011), and 72% in Germany (2013). The median turnout for the national lower house election covered by the study was 69% (very typical), but the mean is 63% (somewhat low).

In each of these five countries, we selected two regions: Quebec and Ontario in Canada, Lower Saxony and Bavaria in Germany, Zurich and Lucerne in Switzerland, Catalonia and Madrid in Spain, and Île-de-France and Provence (sometimes labelled "PACA" for Provence à Côte d'Azur) in France.[3] We selected regions that differ in their party systems, with the constraint that the region had to be populous enough that we could obtain a relatively large sample (about 1,000) of respondents in each case. We selected two regions within each country because we wanted to compare subnational and national elections.

We thus have ten cases, that is, two regions in each of our five countries. In two countries (France, Germany, and Spain), we cover three separate elections: supranational (the European 2014 election), the national election for the lower house, and subnational.[4] In Canada, Spain, and Switzerland, we examine the national and the most important subnational election, which we call "regional." In Canada, these are provincial elections, in Switzerland cantonal elections, in Germany state (Lander) elections, and in Spain (autonomous) regional elections. In the case of France, we selected municipal instead of regional elections because the former are generally considered to be more important, as indicated by their higher turnout rate.[5]

In the two French regions and in Lower Saxony, we have three elections, while in the two Canadian provinces, the two Swiss cantons, the two Spanish regions, and the Bavarian state there are two elections. And we have the additional case of British Columbia for the 2015 Canadian election. This yields a total of twenty-four elections in eleven different regions. Note that in the case of national and supranational elections, the two elections that we examine in two different regions are part of the same election. We therefore have seventeen "independent" elections. As the region is the common unit of analysis, we systematically refer to twenty-four elections.[6]

Except for Bavaria and the 2015 Canadian election, the MEDW survey consisted of a pre-election wave with about 1,000 respondents (usually in the last ten days of the campaign) and about 750 respondents (out of the initial 1,000) in the post-election wave (usually in the seven days following the election). The pre-election wave took about twenty minutes and the post-election wave about ten minutes. We use the post-election wave for the dependent variable (whether the person voted or not) and the pre-election wave for the main independent variables (the four attitudes).

In the case of the 2015 Canadian election, we drew larger samples in each of the three provinces. In the end, we had 1,879, 1,891, and 1,849 respondents in the pre-election wave in British Columbia, Ontario, and Quebec, respectively, and 1,195, 1,308, and 1,206 in the post-election wave. In the case of Bavaria, we have a special three-wave panel, with the first wave occurring just before the September 15, 2013, regional election, the second wave right after and right before the September 22 national election, and the third and last wave immediately after the national election. The sample sizes for these waves were 4,261, 3,575, and 2,895, respectively.

Table A.1 of Appendix 2 summarizes the information about each of the twenty-four elections. The mean turnout in the twenty-four elections is 61% and the median 58%. The five Canadian elections are single-member district plurality elections, while the Swiss and the Spanish elections are proportional representation (PR) elections. The German national and state elections are mixed compensatory (with two votes) while the German European elections are PR. Finally, the voting system varies across the three levels in France: the French European election is held under PR, the national legislative election is single-member district two-round (majority/plurality), and municipal elections are held under a two-round mixed system that guarantees the winning list an absolute majority of seats, which can be considered mixed majoritarian.[7]

The main dependent variable throughout the book is whether the person voted or not. This information is provided in the post-election survey. In fact, there was a wording experiment. The first sentence of the turnout question was identical for all respondents: "In each election we find that a lot of people were not able to vote because they were not registered, they were sick, or they did not have time." This sentence is meant to make it easier for people to admit that they did not vote.[8]

Half of the respondents (the control group) were then simply asked, "Were you personally able to vote in this election?" with the response categories being "yes," "no," and "don't know." The other half (the treatment group) were asked instead, "Which of the following best describes you?" with the response categories being: "I did not vote in the election," "I thought about voting but didn't this time," "I voted in the election," and "don't know." In both cases, we assume that "don't know" corresponds with abstaining. As expected, the treatment version facilitates the admission of abstention and yields a lower turnout (Morin-Chassé et al. 2017). We have merged the two versions in all the analyses reported below. In Table A.2 of Appendix 2, we show that the patterns remain the same with the two versions of the question. The only interaction that is significant is related to "care." The substantial difference should not be overstated, however. Concretely, going from 1 standard deviation below the mean in care to 1 above the mean has an impact of 13 percentage points in the treatment group compared with 8 percentage points in the control group, for a net difference of 5 points.

The MEDW data are based on online quota-based surveys that guarantee the representativeness of the samples with respect to gender, age, education, and region. Like almost every survey, the reported turnout is much higher than the official turnout. This is so first and foremost because of a self-selection bias. Those who are more interested in politics (and more inclined to vote) are more prone to agree to participate in a study that deals with politics. There is, on top of that, a social desirability effect. There is the public norm that the good citizen should feel a moral obligation to vote. For this reason, some people are reluctant to admit that they did not vote, and thus some abstainers indicate that they voted. The consequence is that abstention is almost always underestimated in surveys, and the MEDW surveys are no exception to this rule.

Most of our analyses, as is usually the case, are based on self-reported vote. We would of course prefer to have validated vote, as there is an overrepresentation of respondents saying that they voted (Rogers and Aida 2014; Selb and Munzert 2013). Does this introduce a major bias? We do not believe so. In a recent study, Chris Achen and André Blais (2016) use the 1980, 1984, and 1986 American National Election Studies (ANES) to examine the correlates of intention to vote, reported vote, and validated vote. They look at the impact of age, education, interest, duty, care, and party identification on intended, reported, and validated vote. They find that "all of the substantively relevant variables are statistically significant and with the correct sign in all three equations" (200), and that "reported vote is better than intended vote as a proxy for actual turnout" (205); they conclude that "our findings support a circumscribed and qualified endorsement of the current practice of conflating studies of intended vote, reported vote, and validated vote" (207). We recognize, however, that the effects reported in this study are likely to be slightly overestimated.

Throughout the book, we use turnout-weighted data; that is, the data are weighted so that the reported turnout in the survey corresponds

FIGURE 1.1   The funnel of causality

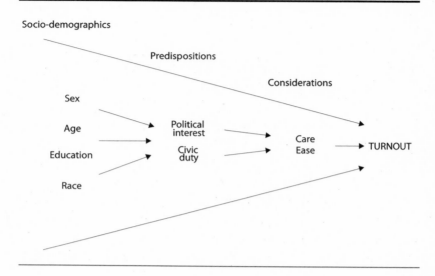

to the official turnout. We do this mostly for descriptive purposes. When we present frequencies or predicted probabilities of voting across different groups, the turnout figures are more realistic this way. This rests on the assumption that the differences in our sample between voters and abstainers are similar to the differences that exist in reality between these two groups.[9] We are assuming that this assumption is approximately correct. In Table A.3 of Appendix 2 we show that the patterns are very much the same with unweighted data.[10]

The analysis is based on a funnel of causality approach (see Campbell et al. 1960; Miller and Shanks 1996; Blais et al. 2002). We start with the most distant factors and then move to consider the more proximate causes. We first examine the socio-demographic correlates of voting, then the two basic predispositions (interest and duty), and finally the two election-specific considerations (care and ease). These can be seen as three distinct "blocs." (See Figure 1.1.)

In each case, we first present descriptive information about the factor (for example, duty) that is the focus of the chapter. Second, we look at the correlations between this factor and the antecedent variables (in the case of duty, socio-demographic characteristics and political interest). The factor is then analyzed as the dependent variable. In a third step, the goal is to ascertain how that factor, now construed as independent variable, affects the propensity to vote, controlling for the antecedent variables. In all these analyses, all the variables are at the individual level, but we are also controlling for the specificities of each case using elections fixed-effects as we include twenty-three dummies for each election (except the regional election in Lower Saxony, which is the reference category).[11]

The approach is different in the last two chapters of this book. In Chapter 7, we take up an alternative interpretation that voting is in good part a habit. We review the various studies that have attempted to test the habit hypothesis and we show that these studies are not very satisfactory. We propose another test of that hypothesis, based on the plausible assumption that the propensity to have a habit is strongly correlated with age. We infer that if people vote or abstain out of habit, the determinants of the turnout decision should vary over the life cycle; that is, the turnout decision should be more strongly affected by values and attitudes among the youth, who presumably have not yet acquired a habit. Using three different datasets, we show that this is not the case, and we conclude that the habit hypothesis is not compelling. Moreover, we also use a different proxy for habit – whether the respondent always voted or abstained and we still find no evidence to support the habit interpretation.

Chapter 8 deals with contextual effects. As indicated above, the focus in this study is on individual-level determinants of the decision to vote or abstain. Clearly, however, this decision is also affected by contextual-level factors. Our claim is simply that these contextual variables correspond to additional causes of turnout that should be considered in a complete account, but that our basic individual-level model that is explicated in this book accounts for most of the variation. Indeed, as we show in Chapter 8 using a multi-level (mixed-effects logistic regression) model, 94% of the variance is due to differences across individuals and only 6% to contextual differences across the twenty-four elections.[12]

We also pay attention to potential interaction effects, that is, whether interest, duty, care, and ease matter more or less in specific contexts. We do find some interesting interaction effects but they are the exception rather than the norm, and, most importantly, they are very modest. This finding buttresses the claim that our model about the factors that drive the decision to vote or abstain applies in all contexts, at least in well-established democracies where voting is not compulsory.

Most of the empirical evidence that we present is based on the MEDW data. The reason is obvious. As this research was directed by the senior co-author, the survey questionnaires included questions designed to tap each of the four major variables that our motivational model incorporates. Furthermore, we believe that it is crucial to test our model with data collected in many different countries and in many different types of elections. The MEDW data satisfy these two criteria. Using the same dataset throughout the book makes it easier for readers to see how the various findings mesh together.

We do, however, use other datasets when they are required to provide more robust tests of our model. This is particularly the case in the last chapters, when we examine the role of habit and contextual factors that are outside our model.

The analyses presented here are based on cross-sectional survey data. Because our model focuses on the motivation (or lack thereof) to vote, we need to tap citizens' attitudes and relate them to their turnout decision, and survey data are therefore essential. As a consequence, experimental studies are not appropriate for testing our model unless they are complemented by survey data, which is seldom the case.[13] We discuss the limitations of experimental research in this specific respect in Chapters 4 and 7 on duty and habit. That being said, it would be better to have longitudinal panel survey data than cross-sectional survey data. Unfortunately, longitudinal panel survey data about the motivation to vote are almost non-existent, so we have to do with the MEDW cross-sectional survey data.[14]

The two main risks associated with the use of cross-sectional data are the possibility that the observed relationships may be spurious and the possibility of reverse causation. Our model assumes that the decision to vote is driven by two strong predispositions, political interest and sense of civic duty. The risk that the observed relationships between interest or duty and turnout are spurious is reduced if these two attitudes are formed early in life and do not change much over the life cycle. In Chapters 3 and 4, we present and discuss evidence provided by longitudinal panel surveys that support our claim that these two attitudes are indeed quite stable. We also refer to studies that show little rationalization from turnout to duty and interest, that is, there is little evidence that voting makes people more interested in politics.

Finally, with respect to care and ease of voting, the risk of spuriousness is small since we control for powerful predispositions (political interest and duty) as well as age and education. We cannot rule out the possibility of rationalization, though that risk is reduced by the fact that these considerations are measured in the campaign survey.

We would of course prefer to test our model with longitudinal panel survey data, and we hope that future research will move in that direction. We believe, however, that the limitations of the cross-sectional data that we utilized are mitigated in this case because there is good empirical evidence that the attitudes that are at the beginning of the funnel of causality constitute strong and stable predispositions.

Our goal is therefore to propose an elegant and parsimonious model of the individual decision to vote in an election, to show that the MEDW data support that model, and to demonstrate that prior research provides additional support for our argument. We begin our empirical investigation by answering a simple question: Who votes?

2

Who Votes?

As indicated in Chapter 1, our goal is to explain why people do or do not vote. It is not possible, however, to provide a sound explanation of why people do what they do if we do not get the facts right. A good description is a necessary (though not sufficient) condition for a good explanation. We thus begin with some descriptive patterns before we consider the causes of electoral participation.

Indeed, the first question that comes to mind when we study turnout at the individual level is: *Who* votes? "Who" refers to the socio-demographic characteristics of voters and abstainers. Is turnout associated with age, race, gender, education, or income? We wish to know the socio-economic profile of voters and abstainers for many reasons. The first is simple curiosity. We want to know what kinds of citizens are more likely to vote or abstain, just as we are curious to learn what kinds of people get up early or late, are vegetarians, or listen to jazz. Second, knowing who votes should help us understand why they vote or should make us become skeptical about some interpretations. For instance, the fact that the better educated are more likely to vote (see below) makes us suspicious about the rational choice model of turnout, since the better educated should better understand that their own single vote is extremely unlikely to make any difference. The third reason is normative. If some groups are much less prone to vote than others, then voters are a biased sample of the eligible population, and we may legitimately wonder about the biases that this introduces in the policy-making process (see Leighley and Nagler 2014, chap. 6). The fourth reason is that when we examine the impact of attitudes on the decision to vote, as we do in subsequent chapters, we need to control for possible spurious effects, and the most obvious antecedent causes of these attitudes are precisely socio-demographic characteristics.

We focus on two socio-demographic characteristics: age and education. We do so because prior research has shown that these are the two strongest socio-economic correlates of turnout. In their classic book *Who Votes?* Raymond Wolfinger and Steven Rosenstone (1980, 102) conclude that the two most important correlates of voting in the United States are education and age. The more recent *Who Votes Now?* (Leighley and Nagler 2014) pays more attention to income, but the authors recognize that "education still trumps income as a predictor of turnout" (66). They also indicate that the "age-related patterns in turnout confirm previous findings," though they note increases in turnout in the 2004 and 2008 elections among both the youngest and oldest age groups.

These studies deal with the United States, which is in many ways a special case. André Blais (2000) examines the socio-demographic correlates of voting in a merged dataset covering nine countries. He looks at the impact of age, gender, education, income, religiosity, marital status, union membership, and employment (being unemployed, retired, or housewife), and finds that "the two most crucial socio-economic determinants of voting are education and age" (52). All other variables have much weaker effects. Furthermore, Neil Nevitte and colleagues (2009) perform a similar analysis, covering twenty-three countries and thirty-two elections. They include age, education, income, marital status, church attendance, place of residence, unionization, gender, and employment status. The two variables that are statistically significant in the greatest number of elections are age and education.[1]

This does not mean that age and education are the most powerful predictors of turnout in each election. Indeed, Aina Gallego (2015) shows that the educational gap in turnout varies substantially across countries. Our more modest claim is that age and education are the two socio-economic variables with the strongest and most consistent relationships with turnout.

Age

Concentrating on these two socio-demographic characteristics in our analysis enables us to examine their relationship with turnout in greater detail. Wolfinger and Rosenstone (1980) show that the relationship is non-linear, that is, turnout starts declining at over 70 years of age. They point out, however, that once education, sex, and marital status are controlled for, there is no real decline at old age. Furthermore, Leighley and Nagler (2014) find that in more recent elections in the United States the turnout rate of the 76–84 age group is in fact higher than average. Governmental (register-based) data in Denmark indicate, however, that turnout peaks at around 65 years, and then starts declining (Bhatti and Hansen 2012). According to Elections Canada (2012) estimates, the drop in Canada begins only at around age 75. Furthermore, there is some evidence, again based on register-based data, that turnout declines between the ages of 18 and 21, as many people leave their parents' home, and so the relationship between age and turnout is a sort of roller coaster (Bhatti, Hansen, and Wass 2012; Bhatti and Hansen 2012).

To complicate things further, it is not always clear how to interpret age differences in the propensity to vote. The usual interpretation, emphasized by Wolfinger and Rosenstone (1980), is the life-cycle one. This makes a lot of sense. As people grow older, they become more integrated into social and political life, and they are more prone to vote (Milbrath and Goel 1977). At the other end of the life cycle, they may become less integrated (especially if they become widowed), and their level of participation declines.[2]

People of different ages belong to different generations. There is strong evidence that the turnout decline that has occurred in most democracies around the end of the twentieth century is in good part a generational effect, that is, the turnout rate of youngest citizens is now considerably lower than it used to be. Blais and colleagues (2004) show that the turnout decline in Canada is mostly the result of the younger generations' lower participation. Wass (2007, 2008) presents similar findings for Finland. Moreover, Blais and Rubenson (2013) combine eighty-six election studies conducted in eight countries since the late 1950s and find that, controlling for life cycle effects, the post-boomers (those born after 1960) are more likely to abstain.

The conclusion is that age differences in turnout reflect both life cycle and generational effects. The problem is that these two variables are strongly correlated. This is particularly the case when the analysis pertains to a single point in time. By definition, younger cohorts are younger in age! One solution is to merge surveys undertaken at different points in time, which produce data at different ages for individuals belonging to the same generation, and a weaker correlation between age and generation. Unfortunately, the Making Electoral Democracy Work (MEDW) surveys were conducted over a short span of time, between 2011 and 2015. This makes it impossible to sort out life cycle and generational effects. We thus refer to age effects without being able to decompose into the life cycle and cohort components.

Figure 2.1 shows the mean turnout rate at each age as well as the LOESS estimate line that best represents the relationship. What is most striking is that the relationship appears to be very much linear. There is no indication that participation starts declining at a late age, although the positive slope stagnates at 80.[3] Overall, Figure 2.1 is in line with the finding by Leighley and Nagler (2014) that in recent years the turnout rate in the United States of the 76–84 group is higher than that of the 46–60 group (the reference category). However, as mentioned above, register-based research shows a decline after a certain age. One way to reconcile these divergent results is to note that surveys are likely to underrepresent people with health problems, and that among the healthy, the relationship between age and turnout is mostly linear.[4] Such linearity is of course consistent with a life cycle interpretation.

Our data demonstrate that age is indeed a strong predictor of turnout. Only about 44% (see Figure 2.1.) of the youngest respondents vote in a typical election, and this percentage increases to 79% among

FIGURE 2.1   The relationship between age and turnout

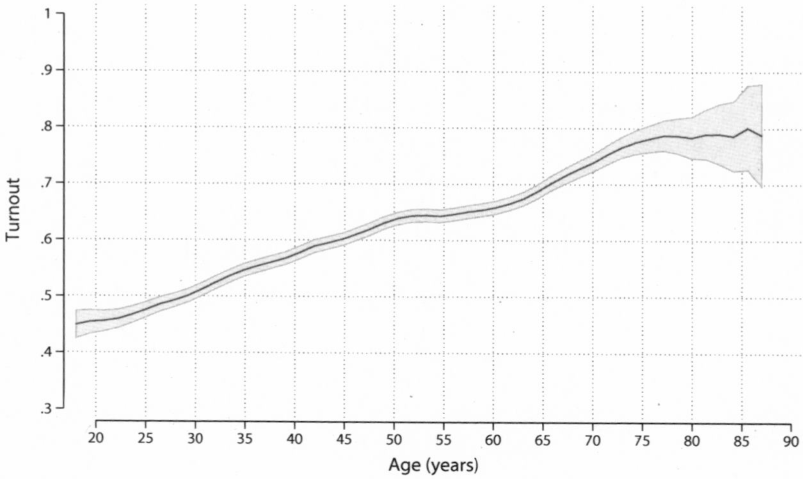

Notes: LOESS regression. Bandwidth = 0.8. The shaded area represents the 95% confidence intervals.

the eldest (or, more plausibly, among the healthy eldest who participate in election surveys).

Education

The second socio-demographic characteristic that we integrate in our model is education. We simply distinguish between those with and without post-secondary education. Forty-seven percent of the respondents have some post-secondary education and are considered as better educated in the following analyses. There is a modest negative correlation between age and education; 60% of those aged 25–34 have some post-secondary education, compared with 43% among those aged 65–74.[5]

When we regress turnout on age and education, each variable is highly significant (see Table 2.1, Model 2).[6] The propensity to vote is 11 percentage points higher when one has some post-secondary education.[7] Furthermore, it is worth noting that there is no interaction effect between age and education.

TABLE 2.1   The determinants of turnout (Models 1–2)

	(Model 1)	(Model 2)
Age	1.87***	2.00***
	(0.12)	(0.13)
Post-secondary education		0.58***
		(0.05)
Constant	−0.43***	−0.58***
	(0.05)	(0.06)
Observations	26,105	26,105
Pseudo R^2	.056	.068

Notes: Entries are logistic regression coefficients. Robust standard errors, clustered by election, are in parentheses. Election fixed effects are included.
* $p < .05$, ** $p < .01$, *** $p < .001$

Conclusion

These first results are easy to summarize. Age and education are not strongly correlated with each other, but they are important independent predictors of voters' propensity to vote or not. This is not surprising, and it is in line with previous findings. This highlights the importance of controlling for these two socio-demographic characteristics throughout the analyses to reduce the possibility of an omitted-variable bias.[8]

The data appear to suggest that age matters more than education since the turnout rate of the eldest is about 30 points higher than that of the youngest, while the gap between the better and the lesser educated is "only" 10 points. This is an unfair comparison, however, since the contrast in the case of age is between extreme (and small) groups, whereas for education it is between two equally large groups. In fact, if we make a simple distinction between those younger than 45 and those aged 45 and over, the age gap is about the same as the education gap.

As mentioned above, it is important to keep in mind that the age gap reflects two effects, life cycle and generational, which we are not able to sort out in this study. Our goal is simply to control for them when we examine the impact of attitudinal factors. The same applies in fact to education. It remains an open question whether the association between education and electoral participation reflects the impact of education as such or rather that of antecedent factors such as childhood socialization and cognitive abilities that make one become more educated (see Persson 2014). We cannot resolve that issue in this research.

3

Do I Like Politics?

According to our model, the decision to vote or not to vote in an election reflects first and foremost how much or how little someone likes politics. The issue is how much or how little a person likes politics, and not how much she likes or dislikes it. Of course, those who dislike politics do not like it, but it does not really matter whether one dislikes politics or is completely indifferent. What is required for turnout is a general positive feeling towards politics.

We thus start with political interest, which we take to signal a basic positive orientation towards politics as a domain of activity. We assume that each of us, for reasons that cannot be examined here, develops an interest or disinterest in politics, as we do for other domains such as religion, sports, or arts. We also assume that political interest or lack of it develops early in life and is stable over time. We assume that the driving motivation is one's basic *affective* orientation towards politics, whether one "finds politics intrinsically interesting" (Hibbing and Theiss-Morse 2002, 130) or not. We refer to "liking" politics rather than "being interested" in politics to stress the affective motivation that drives people to follow or avoid politics the way they do other domains, such as sports or religion.

This assumption relies in good part on Markus Prior's masterful study (2019) of political interest, in which he makes several important points. At the conceptual level, he notes that "affective elements of political interest include excitement and absence of boredom" (21), and "at its core, interest is about the initial affective reaction, often just a diffuse emotion of liking and enjoyment" (36). We therefore equate interest in politics with liking politics and lack of interest with not liking it.

Prior's study systematically documents the remarkable stability of political interest at the aggregate level, both across countries and over time. In Germany, the fall of the Berlin Wall produced an increase in political interest of about 10 percentage points among West Germans, but the change was temporary as the aggregate level reverted to its prior level. Similarly, East Germans' level of political interest was exceptionally high in 1990 but it dropped by more than 10 points in the following two years. There was no noticeable movement in the next twenty years. There is even greater stability in Britain, where political interest "changed very little over last thirty years" (Prior 2019, 93). Prior also notes that aggregate levels everywhere are typically close to the scale midpoint.

Prior's 2010 article documents the stunning stability of political interest at the individual level. The conclusion is crystal clear: "In the absence of extraordinary political upheaval, political interest among citizens looks like a stable personal characteristic with only a few fleeting ups and downs. And when, for whatever reason, people are more (or less) interested than usual, they return to their personal equilibrium level of interest within a year, if not more quickly" (763). Prior adds one qualification in his book (2019, 150): "Among teenagers, political interest is not yet stable. Stability rises rapidly as people approach their twenties, and in their early thirties most of them have conclusively decided how interesting they find politics." The bottom line and the most interesting conclusion for our study, however, is that among those who have the right to vote (those aged 18 and above), namely, those we are concerned with, one's level of interest in politics can be considered a stable personal characteristic.

Prior (2019, chap. 3) presents encouraging findings with respect to the measurement of political interest. Most importantly, he shows that question wording does not seem to matter much: "Survey questions appear to measure the same kind of interest regardless of whether they ask about 'politics,' 'information about government and politics,' 'public affairs and government,' 'social issues in your country,' or 'environmental issues.'" Furthermore, "the strong correlations between different interest questions, the emergence of a dominant first dimension in factor analyses, and the associations between single-item measures and many relevant outcomes all demonstrate that understanding general political interest means understanding much about political interest" (60). In short, simply asking people how interested they are in politics provides a valid and reliable indicator of how much they like politics.

We use the presence or absence of political interest as an indicator of how much one does or does not like politics, of how much one finds political matters exciting or boring, and of how much or how little one is motivated to follow and participate in politics. There is of course the possibility that the development of political interest is shaped by resources. According to this perspective, those without the required resources to participate in politics are not attracted to the political domain and become less interested in politics.

Some of the findings reported by Prior (2019) suggest that resources are not crucial in the development, or lack thereof, of political interest. Perhaps the most central resource of all is educational attainment. As we show below, there is a correlation between education and political interest, but Prior's analyses (2010, 245) indicate that the causal effect of education is limited: "Education has some detectable effects on political interest, but the magnitude of many of these effects is not large and they often do not last long. The strongest claim of unambiguous and durable effects of education on political interest arises for secondary schooling. Vocational and university education have minimal impact on political interest."

The verdict is even more clearly negative with respect to more specific economic resources: "After accounting for educational attainment, other components of socioeconomic status, including income and type of employment, do little to explain political interest ... Raising poor people's income, making sure they have jobs, and seeing them move into high-status occupations would reduce their economic hardship – but it would do nothing to make them more interested in politics" (Prior 2019, 289).

Prior's study provides strong support for construing a person's general level of political interest as a personal and stable predisposition that is the starting point for understanding why a person decides to vote or abstain in an election. The study also suggests that one's level of political interest can be tapped through one simple and direct question. The Making Electoral Democracy Work (MEDW) surveys include a simple question asking respondents to rate their general level of interest in politics on a scale from 0 to 10, where 0 means "not interested at all" and 10 means "a great deal of interest."[1] This is the measure of political interest, which is the focus of this chapter. This variable, like all the variables included in the various analyses reported in this book, is recoded from 0 to 1.

The mean interest level in our sample is .63. The modal category, with 17% of the responses, is .8. The standard deviation is .27. The overall level of political interest is relatively high but there is quite a bit of variance. The level of interest may be somewhat overestimated because there is probably a social desirability bias, as some individuals may be reluctant to admit that they are not interested (the good citizen should be interested in as many things as possible). Furthermore, there is bound to be a selection bias, as those who are not interested in politics are less likely to agree to participate in an election survey (Groves, Presser, and Dipko 2004).[2]

Prior (2019) reports that the aggregate level of political interest appears to be quite similar across countries, and we therefore do not expect much difference across the five countries covered by the MEDW surveys. Figure 3.1 confirms this expectation. Mean interest is close to the total mean (.62) in each of the five countries. It is slightly higher in Germany (.66) and slightly lower in Spain (.60), but the differences are minimal.

Moreover, if Prior is right that political interest is stable, we should not see much variation in political interest as reported at the time of different levels of elections. This is exactly what the data show (Figure 3.1). The mean level of reported general interest in politics is the

FIGURE 3.1   Political interest by country and level of election

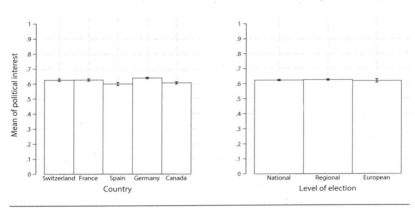

Note: The 95% confidence intervals are included.

TABLE 3.1   The determinants of interest

	(Model 1)
Age	0.32***
	(0.02)
Post-secondary education	0.09***
	(0.01)
Constant	0.53***
	(0.01)
Observations	26,105
R^2	.072

Notes: Entries are ordinary least squares (OLS) regression coefficients. Robust standard errors, clustered by election, are in parentheses. Election fixed effects are included.
* $p < .05$, ** $p < .01$, *** $p < .001$

same (.62) at the time of supranational, national, or subnational elections, even if turnout in supranational elections is much lower.

We now take political interest as the dependent variable and we examine how it is related to age and education in Table 3.1. Without much surprise, we find that those who are older and who are better educated tend to be more interested in politics. All in all, interest is

.08 higher on the 0-to-1 scale among those who have some post-secondary education. As expected, the correlation is not very strong. The impact of age is about the same magnitude. If we compare a 60-year-old individual with a 30-year-old one, the predicted interest gap between the two is .09 on the same 0-to-1 scale.[3]

How strongly is interest correlated with turnout? The answer is: very strongly. Figure 3.2 shows the bivariate relationship between interest and turnout. We can see that turnout is 26% among those with a score of 0 and 76% among those with a score of 1. What is even more striking is that the relationship is very much linear. With one exception (those with a score of .1), turnout increases by about 5 percentage points for each increment of .1 on the political interest score, which produces a 50-point turnout gap between the two extremes. While the relationship is very strong, it is far from perfect, as about a quarter of those with no interest at all vote and a quarter of those with huge interest abstain. This leaves room for other factors to play a part.

FIGURE 3.2   The bivariate relationship between political interest and turnout

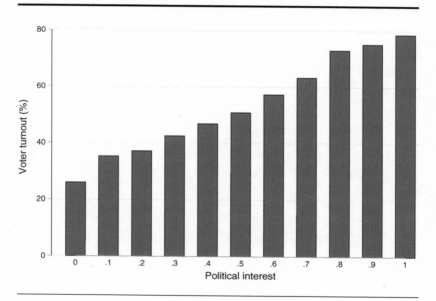

However, we need to control for age and education to ascertain the specific independent effect of political interest on turnout. The estimation from a logistic regression model is presented in Table 3.2 (Model 3). Figure 3.3 shows the predicted probability of voting for various degrees of political interest, keeping age and education constant. We see that the likelihood of voting increases from 28% to 75%, a 47-percentage-point difference, as the level of interest shifts from 0 to 1. These numbers are very similar to those presented in Figure 3.2, which indicates that controlling for age and education does not substantially alter the findings. A more appropriate contrast would be between an individual at .3 (low level) and one at .9 (high level), and then the difference is 30 points (41% versus 71%).[4]

All in all, there are huge variations in individuals' level of interest in politics. These variations are related to age and education, but not too strongly. These variations matter a lot. The propensity to vote increases substantially and systematically as one's political interest increases.

FIGURE 3.3   The impact of political interest on turnout

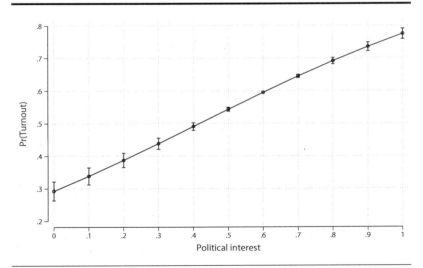

Notes: Predicted probabilities based on Model 3 of Table 3.2. The 95% confidence intervals are included.

TABLE 3.2   The determinants of turnout (Models 1–3)

	(Model 1)	(Model 2)	(Model 3)
Age	2.15***	2.29***	1.73***
	(0.13)	(0.14)	(0.17)
Post-secondary education		0.58***	0.41***
		(0.05)	(0.05)
Political interest			2.28***
			(0.12)
Constant	−0.43***	−0.58***	−1.85***
	(0.05)	(0.06)	(0.07)
Observations	26,105	26,105	26,105
Pseudo R^2	.056	.068	.124

Notes: Entries are logistic regression coefficients. Robust standard errors, clustered by election, are in parentheses. Election fixed effects are included.
$^*\, p < .05,\, ^{**}\, p < .01,\, ^{***}\, p < .001$

This relationship holds across age and educational groups. The decision to vote or not to vote is very much shaped by whether people like politics or not. For people who like politics, voting is the "normal" thing to do. For people who do not like politics, the temptation to stay home is strong.

As people's level of interest in politics is stable over time, especially after young adulthood, one implication is that the most interested tend to vote in most elections while the least interested are prone to abstaining. If interest is a strong predictor of turnout and if interest does not change over time, electoral participation is bound to be stable as well. Such stability may give the impression that voting or abstaining is a habit, but it may simply reflect the fact that people's attitudes, which shape their turnout decision, do not change. We tackle this question directly in Chapter 7.

For the time being, the main message is that citizens have different tastes for politics, that these tastes are stable, and that people are much more likely to vote if they find politics interesting. This is not the whole story, as quite a few of those who are very interested in politics do not vote in some elections, and quite a few of those who are not interested at all make a special effort to go to the polls at least some of the time. We thus need to consider other factors. The following chapter examines another important attitude: whether people believe that they have a moral duty to vote.

4

Do I Have a Duty to Vote?

Democracy is very much about allowing citizens the freedom to express their views. In principle, that freedom should extend to allowing people the right not to express their views if they so wish. Citizens should have the right to vote, but also not to vote.

Yet, voting is made compulsory in many countries (Singh 2019). There is thus also the belief that voting is not only a right but also a duty. Even in countries where voting is voluntary, public authorities often express the view that even if people are not legally obliged to vote they still have a duty to go to the polls. This is well illustrated by the US Citizenship and Immigration Services document *Citizenship Education and Naturalization Information,* which states that "the right to vote is a duty as well as a privilege" (Dalton 2008, 28).

Many citizens share the view that even if people are legally free to abstain, they have a duty to vote. Indeed, overwhelming majorities in Canada and Britain agree with the statement that it is the duty of every citizen to vote (Blais 2000, 95; Clarke et al. 2004, 251). Similarly, when Americans are asked how important, on a scale from 1 to 7, it is for the good citizen to always vote in elections, they give a mean score of 6.2, just a little lower than obeying the laws and not evading taxes (Dalton 2008, 30).

There is thus the public norm, even in places where voting is formally free, that democratic citizenship entails a moral obligation to vote. It is easy to see that the public authorities have an interest in propagating that norm. If people believe that they have a duty to vote, turnout will be higher (see below), and a higher turnout may contribute to enhancing the legitimacy of the system.[1] But there is clearly more than that.

The basic argument supporting the view that voting is a civic duty is that democracy entails both rights and duties and that "all members of the community have a duty to contribute to collective decision-making if they are to enjoy its fruits" (Birch 2009, 42). The belief in the duty to vote is predicated on the idea that one should contribute to the collectivity by, at the minimum, participating in elections. On the one hand, elections are construed as being a central and indeed necessary component of democracy (democracy cannot exist without elections).[2] On the other hand, voting is not a demanding activity (see Chapter 6) and so it seems reasonable to ask citizens to devote at least a little bit of effort to this collective decision.

There are good reasons to construe voting as a duty that a good citizen should fulfill, but there are also good reasons to believe that people should be free to abstain if that is their choice. Many people spontaneously subscribe to the two views. As mentioned above, most people agree with the statement that it is a citizen's duty to vote in elections; at the same time, most people believe that "in a democracy, people should have the right to vote, but also the right to abstain."[3]

There are thus two legitimate views about how to construe voting. The question is whether people have personally internalized the belief that they have a moral obligation to vote in elections. If they have internalized that norm, they should have a greater propensity to cast a vote.

It is important to distinguish duty from interest-based motivation. In the latter case, one votes because she *wants* to. She likes politics and she is keen to participate in the political process in general and in elections particularly. In the case of duty, the person votes because she *should*. The driving force is not her feelings (whether she likes politics or not) but her conscience, which tells her that voting is good, abstaining is bad, and she should do what is right. Duty is a normative (moral) judgment, which belongs to the domain of ethics. The dutiful does not attempt to maximize her personal utility; she wants to make the "right" decision. Our model is thus predicated on the presence of two distinct motivations (or lack thereof): the desire to vote (she wants to) because she likes politics, and the sense of obligation to vote (she ought to) because of her moral belief.

We construe sense of civic duty as a strong and stable personal predisposition, in the same way as political interest. In the case of political interest, as indicated in the previous chapter, we have strong empirical evidence that it is remarkably stable over time. The evidence regarding civic duty is more limited, but at least four studies suggest a similar degree of stability.

First, André Blais and Chris Achen (2019) measure duty (with the duty/choice question; see below) three times in January, March, and October 2008, before the 2008 US presidential election, and a fourth time right after the election. The authors report a high level of stability. Second, Carol Galais and André Blais (2014) use a panel survey conducted in Spain in four waves over a period of eighteen months between 2010 and 2012, at a time of a deep economic crisis, to determine whether the economic crisis had an impact on sense of civic duty (measured through the duty/choice question). They conclude that "the effect of the economic crisis in the evolution of the civic duty to vote is quite modest and confined to the youngest segment of the population ... adhesion to civic responsibilities survives even in a country experiencing very hard times" (6–7).

Third, Galais and Blais (2016a) use the same Spanish data as well as a two-wave panel survey conducted in Canada to estimate a cross-lagged model for duty and turnout. The main goal of the article is to determine whether there is any evidence of rationalization, that is, turnout having an impact on sense of civic duty. The authors find no evidence of rationalization in Spain and some weak trace of it in Canada, the latter results being less robust because they are based on only two waves. But perhaps most importantly for our purposes, their estimations show stronger over-time stability for sense of civic duty than for reported turnout. Fourth, Fernando Feitosa and Carol Galais (2019) examine the stability of civic duty (measured through responses to an agree/disagree statement that "I would be seriously neglecting my duty as a citizen if I didn't vote") over five waves of the 2005–10 British Election Panel Study. Feitosa and Galais find a strong degree of over-time stability. All these studies support the view that sense of civic duty is a deeply held personal belief that is relatively impervious to change.

Most importantly, there is also strong evidence that holding such a belief enhances the propensity to vote. The presence of a close association between civic duty and turnout has been known for a long time. From its very inception, the American National Election Study included a battery of questions to tap sense of citizen duty, and the authors of both *The Voter Decides* (Campbell, Gurin, and Miller 1954) and *The American Voter* (Campbell et al. 1960) mention the strong correlation between duty and the likelihood of voting.

From a different perspective, William Riker and Peter Ordeshook (1968) find it necessary to include a "*D*" term for duty in their calculus of voting model. Interestingly, their own data (table 3) indicate that duty has a more powerful influence on the propensity to vote than the other two central variables (benefits and probability).[4] In *To Vote or Not to Vote?* Blais (2000) presents evidence that sense of duty has an independent effect on turnout, even after controlling for political interest and rational choice considerations such as differential benefits (the "*B*" term in Riker and Ordeshook 1968), the perceived probability of being pivotal (the "*p*" term) and the expected cost of voting (the "*C*" term). The author also provides qualitative evidence that many people spontaneously refer to a sense of civic duty when asked why they vote, and demonstrates that feeling or not feeling that there is a moral obligation to vote shapes the considerations that influence the decision to vote or abstain. More specifically, those who believe that they have a duty to vote are mostly insensitive to "rational" factors such as the cost of voting.

All these studies are based on cross-sectional data. There is the risk that causation goes in the opposite direction – that once people have decided to vote or abstain, they come to believe that they have or do not have a duty to vote – but panel studies have shown little (Galais and Blais 2016a) or no (Blais and Achen 2019) evidence of such rationalization. Blais and Achen (2017) find that duty measured in January strongly predicts the decision to vote or abstain in November. Galais and Blais (2016a) report that duty measured in the previous wave is associated with turnout, even after controlling for previous turnout. All these findings support the claim that sense of civic duty is a stable motivation that powerfully affects the decision to vote or abstain.

Ideally, we would like to have experimental data to better isolate the causal effect of civic duty. It is difficult to see how we could manipulate people's sense of duty, however, especially given that it is a deeply held belief that is relatively impervious to change. The bottom line is that the only way to ascertain the impact of an attitude such as sense of duty is to rely on survey data, while using panel data to measure its stability and to correct for potential rationalization effects.[5]

Many field experiments have been conducted to ascertain the impact of various factors that may affect turnout. Some of these experiments have dealt with the influence of social pressure and have examined, directly or indirectly, the role of civic duty. Perhaps the best known is that of Allan Gerber and colleagues (2008).

This study is a large-scale field experiment conducted at the time of the 2006 Michigan statewide primary election. The researchers test the impact of four different messages sent by mail by an unknown consulting firm during the campaign. All four messages started and ended with the sentence "DO YOUR CIVIC DUTY AND VOTE!" They were thus designed to appeal to citizens' sense of duty and encourage them to vote. The first message, called the "civic duty" treatment, did not include any other consideration. The second treatment ("Hawthorne") informed people that they were being studied and that there would be an analysis of public records. The third treatment ("self-treatment") informed them that who votes is a matter of public record, that the firm had collected data about their household turnout in previous elections and that it would update the data after the election. The fourth treatment ("neighbours") provided the same information about neighbours so that "you and your neighbours will all know who voted and who did not."

The authors report that turnout was 2, 3, 5, and 8 percentage points higher in the four experimental groups than in the control group. They conclude that "these findings demonstrate the profound importance of social pressure as an inducement to political participation" (Gerber, Green, and Larimer 2008, 33). These results are often interpreted as implying that social pressure is a much more powerful factor than civic duty, but this interpretation is unwarranted.

We should keep in mind that there would be no social pressure in the absence of a public norm that the good citizen has a duty to vote. Presumably those who vote because they are concerned that their neighbours will know whether they voted or not do so because they are aware that many people believe that the good citizen should vote, and they want their neighbours to think that they are good citizens. The question, then, is who has, and who has not, internalized the norm. Presumably those who have internalized the norm and believe that they have a duty to vote should vote regardless of social pressure, and those who have rejected the norm and believe that voting is a matter of personal choice should also be little influenced by what others will think. Those who are ambivalent or have no view about this should be most sensitive to being reminded that their turnout record will be made public.

Indeed, it is not at all surprising that the civic duty message as such had little impact. After all, this was a message that most people had presumably heard many times, and one about which most people had already formed relatively strong and stable views, as we have seen previously. Reading about the duty to vote one more time is unlikely to convince people to go to the polls, except perhaps among the ambivalent. Our interpretation of Gerber and colleagues' findings (2008) is thus that they confirm that civic duty is a stable belief, which is difficult to shake. As James Druckman and Thomas Leeper (2012, 889) have shown, "the nonexistence of an experimental effect may stem from a large number of individuals forming strong attitudes ... in response to earlier communications, prior to the experiment."

What about social pressure? Clearly the fact that a single message in the mail could increase turnout by 8 percentage points is stunning, and this undoubtedly shows that social pressure works. That impact may reflect the effect of other factors as well, though. Not only were people told that their neighbours would know whether they voted but they realized that an unknown consulting firm was collecting data about them and their local community, and this must have raised all kinds of concerns other than social pressure.

What is also clear is that the type of social pressure examined in this field experiment is very odd. It is safe to assume that people take for granted that their neighbours are not aware of their turnout decision. All of a sudden, people in the "neighbour treatment" group were told that voting records are public, that a consulting firm was collecting data about them, and that their neighbours would be informed. All this is most unusual and explains in good part why the message had so much impact. But this is very different from the kind of social pressure that people are submitted to in real life outside this field experiment. The persons who may know about our turnout decision and who may directly or indirectly exert some pressure on us are spouses, relatives, and friends (Blais et al. 2019).

In short, this experiment clearly demonstrates that people are sensitive to social pressure when they make up their mind whether to vote or not. We cannot tell, however, how frequent or infrequent social pressure is and how influential the more usual soft pressure (which is the most common in real life) is. Experiments such as that of Gerber and colleagues (2008) are extremely interesting, but to fully appreciate the role of social pressure we need good, old-fashioned(!) descriptive survey evidence about whether people are asked whether they will vote or have voted, whether they think that their friends and relatives know about their decision, and whether they care about this. The little empirical evidence that we do have suggests that there is in fact very little social pressure outside the household (Blais, Galais, and Coulombe 2019). Most importantly, finding that a duty message has no impact in a field experiment in no way means that sense of civic duty has little or no effect on the turnout decision, since feelings of duty precede reception of a duty message.

We examine below the effect of civic duty on the propensity to vote, after controlling for one's level of political interest. Even though political interest and civic duty are conceptually distinct, we expect them to be empirically correlated. Those who like politics are more likely to think that elections are important and that they have a moral obligation to participate. Conversely, those who do not like politics should be more prone to believe that there are many things more important in life than elections, and to conclude that abstaining is all right. As we show below, however, that correlation is not very strong. There are quite a few respondents who love politics but think that there is nothing wrong with deciding to abstain at least some of the time, and quite a few who do not care much about politics but believe that they have a moral obligation to vote. It is therefore possible to sort out the specific impact of duty, independent of interest, and vice versa.

We suppose that in every society there are some people whose moral conscience tells them that they ought to vote because this is the right thing to do; others who feel that it is a matter of choice and so they feel free to vote or abstain, depending on the circumstances; and still others who do not have clear views on the matter but are prone to pay lip service to the public norm that it is a civic duty to vote even though they do not truly personally adhere to that norm. The challenge is to neutralize as much as possible the social desirability effect associated with the presence of a public norm in order to tap citizens' true feeling about whether or not voting is a duty.

Blais and Galais (2016) have proposed a battery of questions to measure the civic duty to vote. They define the civic duty to vote as the belief that one has a moral obligation to vote in elections, insisting on the fact that the motivation is *moral* in nature; the person believes that voting is the right thing to do and that abstaining is wrong. They argue that this moral component should be reflected in the questions that are used to tap civic duty. They also insist on the importance of paying attention to the risk of social desirability and of avoiding as much as possible agree/disagree questions, which can be plagued with social desirability and acquiescence biases (Krosnick 1999; Schuman and Presser 1981; Saris et al. 2010). Blais and Galais (2016) go on to propose a long battery of fourteen questions and a short one of four questions.

This proposal came long after the Making Electoral Democracy Work (MEDW) questionnaire was constructed. Fortunately, two of the four questions included in the Blais/Galais short battery were part of the MEDW questionnaire. The first duty/choice question is as follows:

> Different people feel differently about voting. For some, voting is a DUTY. They feel that they should vote in every election however they feel about the candidates and parties. For others, voting is a CHOICE. They feel free to vote or not to vote in an election depending on how they feel about the candidates and parties. [The order of these two statements was varied randomly.]
>
> For you personally, voting is FIRST AND FOREMOST a:
> □ Duty
> □ Choice
> □ Don't know

There was a follow-up question for those who answered "duty," about whether they felt very strongly, somewhat strongly, or not very strongly that voting was a duty. This allows us to create a choice/duty scale from 0 (for those who do not select duty initially) to 1 (for those who feel very strongly that they have a duty to vote).

This question has the advantage of not being an agree/disagree question. Furthermore, since "choice" is a positively loaded term (having a choice is a good thing), the question offers a positive non-duty option and makes it easier for respondents to admit that they do not feel that they have a duty to vote. Indeed, the mean score is around .4 on the 0-to-1 scale.[6]

The second question is more indirect. People are asked to indicate how guilty (very, somewhat, not very, not at all) they would feel if they did not vote. Again, we created a scale from 0 (not at all guilty) to 1 (very guilty). The logic is simple. Those with a strong sense of civic duty must believe that abstention is morally wrong. They should thus feel guilty if they were to engage in some wrongdoing. Indeed, guilt can be defined as the "feeling associated with the recognition that one has violated a personally relevant moral or social standard" (Kugler and Jones 1992, 318). Following this logic, we tell our friends that if they wish to know whether they have a sense of duty to vote, they just need to imagine how they would feel if they decided to abstain in an election. If they would have no feeling of guilt, they most likely do not really believe that voting is a moral obligation.[7]

When we looked at the distribution of responses to the duty/choice question, we found that German and Swiss respondents were much more inclined to select "choice" than the French, the Spaniards, and the Canadians. This could indicate that sense of duty is weaker in Germany and Switzerland, but there is also the possibility that the difference reflects the absence of linguistic equivalence. This led us to look closely at how the duty/choice question was translated in German (the Swiss questionnaire was also in German).

Duty is translated as "Pflicht," which, according to the German-speaking colleagues we consulted, is straightforward. The translation for "choice" is "bewusste entscheidung," which is more problematic. Literally, this means "conscious decision." It seems that "choice" is a very difficult word to translate into German. Swiss and German respondents were thus asked to indicate whether they construed voting as a duty or a conscious decision, and so implicitly duty was portrayed as an "unconscious" decision. It is thus not surprising that most Swiss and German respondents selected the "conscious decision" option.[8] We are unable to tell whether another German translation would have been more appropriate, but clearly there is an equivalence problem. We therefore decided to use only the guilt question to measure sense of civic duty.

Results

We begin with a description of our duty variable. The mean score in the whole sample is .49. The standard deviation is .37. There are thus

FIGURE 4.1   Duty by country and level of election

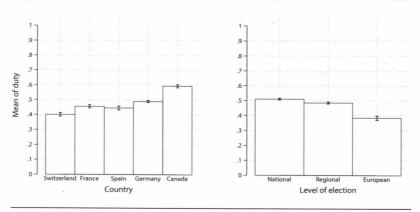

Note: The 95% confidence intervals are included.

substantial individual differences in people's belief that they have a moral obligation to vote in elections. As in the case of interest, we do not expect strong differences in sense of civic duty across the five countries. Figure 4.1 shows that there is one outlier. Canadians are more likely to say that they would feel guilty if they did not vote (mean of .59). The four other countries display a mean between .40 and .48. This difference is confined to the two English-speaking provinces (Ontario and British Columbia), which display a mean level of .65 and .63, while Quebec is not significantly different from the other countries, with a mean of .52.

In a first step, we look at the determinants of duty. Table 4.1 (Model 1) shows that sense of civic duty increases with age and education. Having a post-secondary education increases duty by .08 on the 0-to-1 scale, an increase of 16% relative to the mean. Likewise, a relatively old (60 years) respondent's typical degree of duty is .09 higher than that of a young (30 years) person, a difference of 18% relative to the mean. These effects are neither small nor huge.

We can also see that sense of duty depends somewhat on one's level of interest in politics (Table 4.1, Model 2). If we compare two individuals with the same age and education, one of whom is very interested (with a score of .9) while the other is not very interested (with a score

TABLE 4.1   The determinants of duty

	(Model 1)	(Model 2)
Age	0.23***	0.06
	(0.04)	(0.05)
Post-secondary education	0.10***	0.05***
	(0.01)	(0.01)
Political interest		0.54***
		(0.01)
Constant	0.38***	0.10***
	(0.02)	(0.02)
Observations	26,105	26,105
R^2	.065	.215

Notes: Entries are ordinary least squares (OLS) regression coefficients.
Robust standard errors, clustered by election, are in parentheses. Election
fixed effects are included.
* $p < .05$, ** $p < .01$, *** $p < .001$

of .3), we would expect the former to score .58 and the latter .33 on sense of duty. Not surprisingly, those who like politics are much more inclined to believe that the good citizen ought to vote. At the same time, the correlation is not overwhelming, and it is thus possible to examine the independent effects of these two attitudes.

Model 4 in Table 4.2 shows that sense of duty has a strong independent impact on the propensity to vote, even controlling for age, education, and interest.[9] Figure 4.2 shows the predicted probability of voting for different values of duty, keeping individuals as they are with respect to age, education, and interest. We can see that this probability increases from 34% when duty equals 0 to 83% when it equals the maximum of 1. If we contrast two individuals with values one standard deviation below and above the mean (as the mean is .49 and the standard deviation is .37, this comes to .1 and .85, respectively), the difference is 39 percentage points (39% for low duty and 78% for high duty). This impact is similar in magnitude to that of political interest (see Chapter 3). The propensity to participate in elections is powerfully shaped by these two attitudes.

TABLE 4.2   The determinants of turnout (Models 1–4)

	(Model 1)	(Model 2)	(Model 3)	(Model 4)
Age	2.15***	2.29***	1.73***	1.81***
	(0.13)	(0.14)	(0.17)	(0.17)
Post-secondary education		0.58***	0.41***	0.33***
		(0.05)	(0.05)	(0.06)
Political interest			2.28***	1.26***
			(0.12)	(0.14)
Duty				2.29***
				(0.07)
Constant	−0.43***	−0.58***	−1.85***	−2.24***
	(0.05)	(0.06)	(0.07)	(0.08)
Observations	26,105	26,105	26,105	26,105
Pseudo R^2	.056	.068	.124	.203

Notes: Entries are logistic regression coefficients. Robust standard errors, clustered by election, are in parentheses. Election fixed effects are included.
* $p < .05$, ** $p < .01$, *** $p < .001$

FIGURE 4.2   The impact of duty on turnout

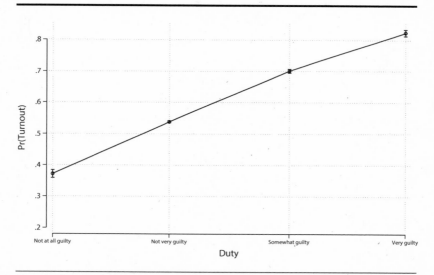

Notes: Predicted probabilities based on Model 4 of Table 4.2. The 95% confidence intervals are included.

Whether one votes or abstains is first a reflection of whether one likes or does not like the world of politics (interest). But it is more than that. Because elections are a central element of democracy, and because there is overwhelming support for the democratic ideal, views about what the good citizen ought to do come into play. Because the democratic ideal puts so much emphasis on freedom, there is the view that people have the right to vote, but also not to vote, in elections. There is also the contrary view that since democracy is a public good that benefits everyone, each citizen has the moral obligation to contribute and that voting constitutes a minimal duty that citizens should fulfill. The civic duty norm is very much present and is often publicly supported by public authorities. Many citizens do not subscribe to this norm and thus feel free not to vote, especially if they are not interested in politics. Many others, however, have internalized the norm and would feel as though they were committing a sin if they were to abstain without good reason. These people feel compelled to vote even if they do not particularly like politics and elections.

5

Do I Care about the Outcome?

The previous two chapters dealt with general attitudes that that predispose people to vote or abstain in most elections. We now consider the proximate considerations (see Figure 1.1) that come into play in specific elections. We test a simple intuition, which is that people are likely to vote when they care about the outcome of the election, whereas they are prone to abstain if they are indifferent.

This consideration is close to the "B" term in the rational choice model. As elaborated by Downs (1957), the citizen tries to predict what policies the various parties or candidates would implement if elected, and estimates the utility she would derive from each. If the differential utility is about nil, it does not make much difference to her who is elected, the expected net benefit is nil or very small, and the logical choice is to abstain. If, on the contrary, who is elected makes an important difference, her differential utility is very high, and she is likely to vote.

We depart from a rational choice perspective since we do not consider the probability that a single vote will be pivotal. According to the rational choice model, people should not vote if they have no preference ($B = 0$) or if they estimate that their own vote will not decide the outcome of the election, that is, the winner will be the same whether they vote or not. André Blais (2000, 2015) has reviewed the empirical evidence elsewhere and shows that the decision to vote or not is *not* substantially affected by the perception that one's single vote could or could not make a difference. In our judgment, this is not a major consideration in the turnout decision, and we do not lose much explanatory power when we leave it aside. Our approach is therefore closer to the expressive model of voting, according to which people vote to express their opinions (Brennan and Buchanan 1984; Brennan and Lomasky 1997; Brennan and Hamlin 1998). The stronger their opinions (the more they care), the greater their willingness to vote.

The question is how much this consideration matters in the decision to vote or abstain. In addressing this issue, it is imperative to consider the general predispositions that we have examined in the previous chapters. If a person likes and follows politics very closely, she is likely to form clear preferences about the issues, the parties, and the candidates, and to be concerned about the outcome of the election. The question then becomes whether being interested in general matters more or less than having a strong preference in a given election. In other words, who is the most likely to vote, the person who has a strong general interest in politics but is not particularly concerned in a specific election, or the person who does not follow politics closely but happens to have a strong preference in a specific election?

We construe "care" to be strongly shaped by individuals' predispositions, most especially by their degree of political interest, but also the specific context of an election. As Mark Franklin (2004) has argued, elections vary in their degree of competitiveness, and that should affect how much people care about the outcome. Some elections are more "important" than others, and we would expect people to be more concerned with the outcome in the most "meaningful" elections. For instance, voters should attach less importance to the elections to the European Parliament than to the elections to the national legislature if they believe that the latter is more powerful than the former. In the same vein, Swiss voters should not care as much about the outcome of elections since many issues are decided by referenda and the government is typically formed by the same "grand" coalition (Franklin 2004, 97; Blais 2014).

We should thus observe greater variation in the overall level of care across elections than in aggregate levels of interest or duty. But judgments about how much or how little an election matters are subjective and hinge on individual predispositions. Those who like politics are bound to find most elections important, whereas those who do not like politics are likely not to be overly concerned most of the time. Contra Franklin (2004, chap. 6), we predict that individual characteristics matter more than election characteristics in shaping judgments about the stakes of an election.

The Making Electoral Democracy Work (MEDW) survey includes a simple and straightforward question: "On a scale from 0 to 10, where 0 means that you don't care at all and 10 means that you care a lot, how much do you care which party will form the government after the election?"[1] The question taps respondents' views about how much or how little is at stake in an election, and about how things may look like afterwards, depending on the outcome. Those who think that the election will not change anything do not have any clear preference and are likely not to care much, while those who believe that the stakes are high will care a lot about the outcome. There are many outcomes associated with an election, but we assume that the outcome that matters most is who forms the government at the end. Indeed, Jean-François Daoust and André Blais (2017) find that voters care more about the national outcome than about the local result in their district, though the gap between the two is relatively small. Hence, we also look at the local outcome (in the district) below.

The motivation that we wish to capture is individuals' feeling about how much an election matters. This is the expressive component of the voting decision. People do or do not have strong views about the parties and the candidates, and the stronger or weaker these views are, the stronger or weaker the willingness to participate in the election. There are several ways to tap this expressive component, and we consider different measures below. We believe, however, that "care" nicely captures both the cognitive and the emotional components of feelings about how much is at stake in an election.

Results

Respondents were invited to use a 0-to-10 scale; the responses were rescaled into a 0-to-1 scale. The mean score is .70, with a standard deviation of .27. Figure 5.1 shows the mean care score by country and type of election. We can see that care is slightly lower in Switzerland and France. In the case of Switzerland, this undoubtedly reflects the fact that elections are less consequential, given the important role played by referenda in deciding specific issues and the presence of grand coalitions. We note, however, that Swiss citizens care only slightly less than citizens of other countries about the outcome of elections. We can also see that voters do not care as much about the outcome of European elections.[2] Regional elections appear to matter as much as national ones, however.[3]

In a first step, we examine the factors that affect how much or little people care about the outcome of the election. Table 5.1 indicates that concern is stronger among the elderly and the better educated. The relationships are not very strong, however. All in all, the predicted score of someone with a post-secondary education is only .05 higher on the 0-to-1 scale. Age matters a little more: the predicted difference

FIGURE 5.1   Care by country and level of election

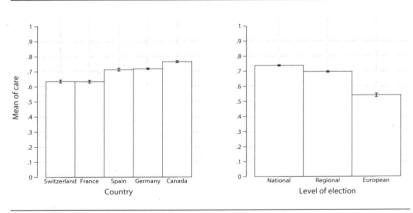

Note: The 95% confidence intervals are included.

TABLE 5.1   The determinants of care

	(Model 1)	(Model 2)	(Model 3)
Age	0.24***	0.08***	0.07***
	(0.02)	(0.02)	(0.01)
Post-secondary education	0.05***	0.00	-0.01
	(0.01)	(0.01)	(0.01)
Political interest		0.50***	0.37***
		(0.01)	(0.01)
Duty			0.25***
			(0.01)
Constant	0.58***	0.32***	0.29***
	(0.01)	(0.01)	(0.01)
Observations	26,105	26,105	26,105
R^2	.097	.329	.415

Notes: Entries are ordinary least squares (OLS) regression coefficients. Robust standard errors, clustered by election, are in parentheses. Election fixed effects are included.
* $p < .05$, ** $p < .01$, *** $p < .001$

between respondents aged 30 and 60 years is .09 point. Age and education have a greater impact on general political interest than on how much one cares about the election. The relationship between care and education disappears after controlling for interest and duty, while the association with age weakens considerably.

As expected, there is a strong correlation between interest and care. For each increment of .1 point in interest there is an increase of .05 point in care (on a 0-to-1 scale), controlling for age and education. The predicted level of care of someone very interested (score of .9) is .3 point higher than that of someone with little interest (score of .3). We also find that those who have a stronger sense of duty are more likely to have stronger preferences, though the effect is weaker than that of interest.

The bottom-line question of this chapter is how much care matters in the turnout decision. In Table 5.2, we can see that whether one cares about the election matters a lot, even controlling for age, education,

TABLE 5.2 The determinants of turnout (Models 1–5)

	(Model 1)	(Model 2)	(Model 3)	(Model 4)	(Model 5)
Age	2.15***	2.29***	1.73***	1.81***	1.73***
	(0.13)	(0.14)	(0.17)	(0.17)	(0.17)
Post-secondary education		0.58***	0.41***	0.33***	0.36***
		(0.05)	(0.05)	(0.06)	(0.06)
Political interest			2.28***	1.26***	0.74***
			(0.12)	(0.14)	(0.15)
Duty				2.29***	1.96***
				(0.07)	(0.06)
Care					1.50***
					(0.19)
Constant	−0.43***	−0.58***	−1.85***	−2.24***	−2.72***
	(0.05)	(0.06)	(0.07)	(0.08)	(0.13)
Observations	26,105	26,105	26,105	26,105	26,105
Pseudo R^2	.056	.068	.124	.203	.217

Notes: Entries are logistic regression coefficients. Robust standard errors, clustered by election, are in parentheses. Election fixed effects are included.
* $p < .05$, ** $p < .01$, *** $p < .001$

interest, and duty. Figure 5.2 shows the predicted probability of voting, everything else being equal, for different values of care. That predicted probability ranges from 55% to 70% as one moves from a score of .5 to 1 on the care question.[4] This is a substantial effect, but it is not as large as that associated with interest and duty.[5]

André Blais and Chris Achen (2019) have argued that the impact of care depends on duty; that is, whether one does or does not care about the outcome of the election matters only among those who do not feel they have a duty to vote. This hypothesis is tested in Table A.4 of Appendix 2 and is confirmed. There is a negative interaction effect between duty and care, which means that care can be construed as a compensatory factor for lack of duty. Those who have a strong sense of duty do not need to care much about the outcome of the election. Care is a more decisive consideration for those who do not believe that

FIGURE 5.2 The impact of care on turnout

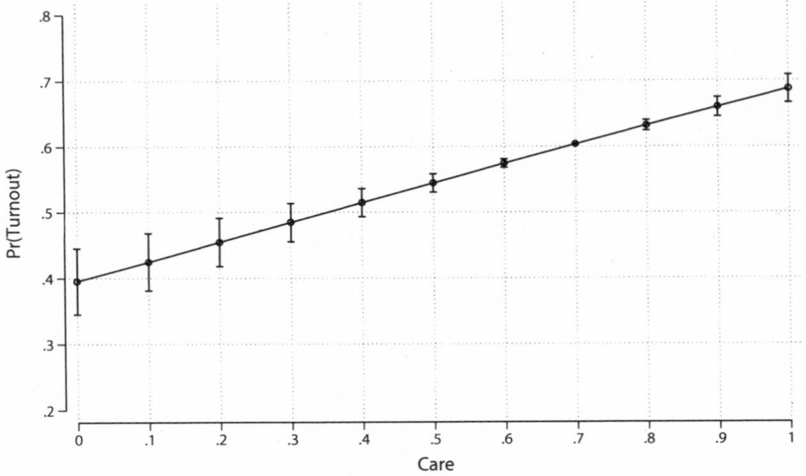

Notes: Predicted probabilities based on Model 5 of Table 5.2. The 95% confidence intervals are included.

they have a moral obligation to vote; they are inclined to abstain unless they conclude that the electoral outcome matters a lot.

In our model, what matters in the decision to vote or abstain is whether the person believes that much hinges on the outcome of the election. The person who thinks that the stakes are low is very much tempted to stay home. The MEDW question therefore asks respondents how much they care about the election. The most significant outcome of the election concerns which party(ies) will form the government; thus, the question taps how much the respondent cares who will form the government.

It could be argued that some people care first and foremost about the outcome of the election in their local district. Even if it is quite rare, some voters support their preferred local candidate even when she is not from their preferred party (Blais and Daoust 2017). Most MEDW surveys did include a "care about who will win in your district" question, also on a 0-to-10 scale.[6] As expected and as shown by

TABLE 5.3 The determinants of turnout: alternative indicators of care

	(Model 1)	(Model 2)
Age	1.50***	1.43***
	(0.19)	(0.15)
Post-secondary education	0.46***	0.35***
	(0.08)	(0.05)
Political interest	0.71***	0.93***
	(0.17)	(0.14)
Duty	1.84***	2.09***
	(0.08)	(0.07)
Care	1.46***	
	(0.26)	
Care (local district)	0.48***	
	(0.12)	
Intensity of preferences		1.21***
		(0.11)
Constant	−2.89***	−2.56***
	(0.17)	(0.10)
Observations	17,454	25,655
Pseudo R^2	.217	.206

Notes: Entries are logistic regression coefficients. Robust standard errors, clustered by election, are in parentheses. Election fixed effects are included.
* $p < .05$, ** $p < .01$, *** $p < .001$

Daoust and Blais (2017), the "local district care" mean score is somewhat lower at .63 (compared with .70 for caring about the government). Furthermore, we note that there is a strong correlation (.49) between caring about who will form the government and caring about who will win the local district. More significantly, if we include both the "government care" and the "district care" indicators in the same estimation, both are significant, but the coefficient associated with the former is much stronger (by about three times), as shown in Model 1 of Table 5.3. We have thus decided to keep the "care about who will form the government" indicator in our analyses.

As mentioned above, the "how much does the election matter?" consideration is conceptually close to the "*B*" term in the rational choice model. In a two-party system, the citizen calculates her utility if party A wins the election (and forms the government) as well as if party B wins, and the differential corresponds to the benefit that is associated with the election. It could thus be argued that the perceived stake in an election could/should be measured by the intensity of preference among the parties.

We thus created a "strength of preference" measure from party ratings that were included in the MEDW surveys. The question wording was: "Please rate each of the following political parties on a scale from 0 to 10, where 0 means you 'really dislike' that party at all and 10 means that you 'really like' that party." Since a preference entails liking one option more than the others, it makes sense to construct a preference indicator on a comparison of how much one likes a party more than the others. Strength of preference simply corresponds to the absolute difference between the most and the least liked party.

We expect strength of preference to be strongly correlated with care, and the correlation is indeed strong (+.41). Why is the correlation not stronger? The reason is likely to be that "preference" tells us about how much some options are better appreciated than others in relative terms. Our "care" variable does capture that relative preference, but it incorporates an additional element, which is the relative salience of the election. It is possible to have a clear preference for a party but not to care that much if the institution to be elected has little power. In short, care reflects strength of preference among the options, weighted by the perceived salience of the election.

Table 5.3 (Model 2) tests whether intensity of preferences has an impact on the decision to vote. As expected, strength of preferences does have an independent effect on the propensity to vote, over and above interest and duty, though this effect is slightly weaker than that of care.

All in all, some people care a lot about the outcome of an election, but some do not care much. There are several ways to capture this feeling, but we believe that the best approach is simply to ask people how much they care about the outcome of the election, and the most salient outcome in parliamentary elections is who forms the government. This feeling is strongly correlated with how much or how little one likes politics and, to a weaker extent, one's sense of civic duty. But there are election-specific factors that come into play as well, and therefore the link between general political interest and the perceived importance of a given election is far from perfect.

We have shown in this chapter that whether one believes that who wins the election makes a difference matters even when general predispositions such as interest and duty are controlled for. This belief, which resembles the "B" term in the rational choice model but also incorporates the perceived salience of the election, clearly affects the propensity to vote. Whether one does or does not care about the outcome does not, however, count as much as general interest in politics or sense of civic duty. Basic and stable predispositions matter the most.

We now move to the fourth and last consideration in our turnout model, which is the perception of how easy or difficult it is to cast a vote.

6

Is It Easy to Vote?

The last consideration in our model is the ease/difficulty of voting. Most people who wish to vote must take the time to go to the polling station, possibly wait in line, make up their mind about their vote choice, and finally cast a vote. How much time does this take? We have little information about this. The only surveys to ask the question, to our knowledge, are surveys conducted at the time of the 1995 Quebec referendum and the 1996 British Columbia election (see Blais 2000, 85).[1] In those surveys, respondents were offered five options: (1) a quarter of an hour, (2) half an hour, (3) three-quarters of an hour, (4) an hour, and (5) more than one hour. Eighty-seven percent of the respondents in both provinces chose the first two options, which suggests that voting does not take much time for most people. Unsurprisingly, two-thirds of respondents said that it was very easy to vote, and less than 10% that it was (somewhat or very) difficult.

Note that these were pre-election surveys that measured how much time people *expected* to take. In the case of Quebec, the same people were re-interviewed after the election and asked how much time it took to vote, and the patterns were similar. There does not seem to be any systematic under- or overestimation in expectations. It is of course expectations that matter, since the decision to vote is influenced by people's perception of how much time it will take, no matter how biased that perception is. These results lead us to believe that few people anticipate that voting will take a lot of time, but we should stress that the information we have concerns only one election and one referendum in two Canadian provinces.

A similar question was asked ten years later in another study conducted in these two provinces. This is a two-wave panel Internet survey conducted by YouGov Polimetrix. The first wave took place in the last week of the September 2008 Canadian federal election among a sample of eligible electors in the provinces of British Columbia and Quebec; the second wave took place in the last week of the December 2008 Quebec provincial election or the May 2009 British Columbia election. The sampling frame was designed to match the demographic profile of each province. The sample size in each province was about 2,000 in the first wave and over 1,000 in the second wave.[2]

In each wave and in each province, the survey included the following question: "For you personally, on a scale from 0 to 10 where 0 means very difficult and 10 means very easy, how easy or difficult is it to go to the polling station?" The mean for each provincial wave varies between 8.5 and 8.7. About 5% gave a score of 3 or lower. These results indicate that people find it quite easy to vote.

In the same vein, several studies in the United States show that distance from the polling station affects turnout (Gimpel, Lay, and Schuknecht 2003; Dyck and Gimpel 2005; Gimpel, Dyck, and Daron 2006). Most interesting is the research by Henry Brady and John McNulty (2011). In the 2003 California recall election, many localities in Los Angeles County consolidated voting precincts, and the polling place for two-thirds of registered voters was changed. The authors compare turnout in the treatment group, using as the control group those whose polling station did not change. They estimate that changing the polling station decreased turnout by 2 percentage points.[3] They also sort out the specific effect of search and transportation, and they find that the former is more important. Distance matters a little but the mere fact of having a new location is more important. This is very interesting but does not tell us much about how easy or difficult it is to vote in a "typical" election.

This discussion assumes that voting takes place in a polling station. This is the case in an overwhelming number of cases, but there are some exceptions. The most important exception is mail voting, and from this perspective Switzerland is a very interesting case since the great majority of people vote by mail. It is fair to assume that voting by mail takes less time than going to a polling station, especially as the person can do it any day (and time) that fits her best, without having to queue. It will be interesting to see whether Swiss respondents are more likely to perceive voting to be easier than those from the other countries.

The Making Electoral Democracy Work (MEDW) survey taps people's perception of the ease or difficulty of voting through a simple and straightforward question: "For some people voting is a simple and easy thing to do. For others, it is difficult or inconvenient. For you personally, how easy or difficult is it to vote?" There are four response categories: very difficult, somewhat difficult, somewhat easy, and very easy. As for the previous considerations, we first look at the distribution of the variable to determine whether most people, as we expect, perceive voting to be quite easy. In the second step, we look at the factors that affect people's perceptions of the ease of voting. Finally, we ascertain how much impact such a consideration has on the turnout decision.

As explained in Chapter 1, we rely on citizens' global *subjective* assessment of the ease of voting. We are interested in subjective perceptions because the individual's decision is necessarily based on them. In prior research, André Blais (2000), following Anthony Downs (1957), distinguished the ease or cost of the act of voting per se, and of the search for information that someone may have to undertake if she wants to vote, in order to determine which party or candidate to vote for. It is not clear, however, that people can readily distinguish these two kinds of cost, and the MEDW team decided to simply tap respondents' overall judgment about how easy or difficult it is to vote.[4]

We are looking at perceptions of the ease/difficulty of voting among those who are already registered. In most countries, it is the state (or some electoral agency) that is responsible for registering new electors (see Massicotte, Blais, and Yoshinaka 2004). In other countries, the

United States being the best-known case, it is up to individuals to take steps to get registered. Getting registered may be very easy or quite difficult, and this varies considerably across countries. We do not have data on this prior step, and we are thus focusing on the decision to vote or abstain for someone who is already registered and who does not have to go through any other procedure (other than possibly proving her identity with an appropriate document) if she wishes to vote.

All in all, 40% of respondents indicated that it is very easy to vote, and another 38% responded that it is somewhat easy; only 4% answered that it is very difficult. We recoded the ease of voting variable on a 0-to-1 scale, with 0 corresponding to very difficult and 1 to very easy. The mean score is .72.

The highest average (i.e., easiest to vote) is observed in Canada (.76) and the lowest in Switzerland (.63). It is somewhat surprising that voting is perceived to be less easy in Switzerland since Swiss citizens have the possibility of voting by mail, which should facilitate the act of voting. Moreover, elections are more frequent. The reason why more people deem voting to be somewhat difficult in Switzerland must be that the presence of many lists and sublists (for youth, seniors, and farmers) makes the ballot (sometime a booklet!) very long, and the possibility of cumulation or panachage (the possibility of supporting candidates from different parties) may render the whole exercise quite complicated. Furthermore, we do not see much difference in the ease of voting across levels of election. The mean is .72 for national elections and .71 for regional and supranational (i.e., European) elections (see Figure 6.1).

It should be noted that, except for Switzerland, the differences across countries (as well as across types of elections) are very small. Voting appears to be a bit easier in Canada than in France, Germany, or Spain, but the similarities clearly trump the differences. There is thus no reason to believe that the Canadian findings reported at the beginning of this chapter about how easy it is to go to the polling station are exceptional.

FIGURE 6.1   Ease of voting by country and level of election

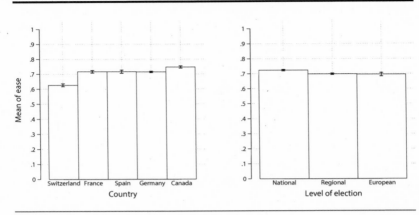

Note: The 95% confidence intervals are included.

TABLE 6.1   The determinants of ease of voting

	(Model 1)	(Model 2)	(Model 3)	(Model 4)
Age	0.27***	0.20***	0.19***	0.19***
	(0.01)	(0.01)	(0.01)	(0.01)
Post-secondary education	0.05***	0.03***	0.02***	0.03***
	(0.01)	(0.01)	(0.01)	(0.01)
Political interest		0.22***	0.17***	0.13***
		(0.01)	(0.01)	(0.01)
Duty			0.11***	0.08***
			(0.01)	(0.01)
Care				0.11***
				(0.01)
Constant	0.63***	0.51***	0.50***	0.47***
	(0.01)	(0.01)	(0.01)	(0.01)
Observations	26,105	26,105	26,105	26,105
R^2	.063	.107	.122	.129

Notes: Entries are ordinary least squares (OLS) regression coefficients. Robust standard errors, clustered by election, are in parentheses. Election fixed effects are included.
* $p < .05$, ** $p < .01$, *** $p < .001$

Table 6.1 shows how the perceived ease of voting is related to age, education, and the three previous considerations. Older and better-educated respondents find it easier to vote but the relationships are not particularly strong. We can also see that those who are interested, who have a sense of duty, and who care about the outcome perceive voting to be easier, with interest having a somewhat larger impact than duty or care. There is, we think, some projection effect. Those who like politics are prone to perceive voting as easy, while those who have little interest are inclined to think that it is not that easy. It should be kept in mind, however, that few people indicate that voting is difficult.

How much of a difference does it make whether voting is deemed to be easy or difficult? Table 6.2 confirms that ease of voting does matter, even controlling for age, education, interest, duty, and care. Figure 6.2 illustrates the impact. The predicted probability of voting increases from 40% to 68% when ease of voting shifts from minimum

FIGURE 6.2   The impact of ease of voting on turnout

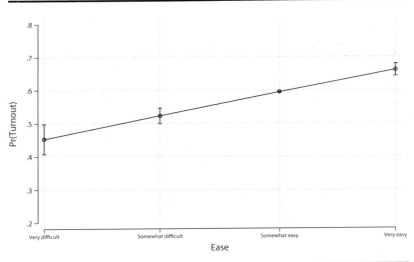

Notes: Predicted probabilities based on Model 6 of Table 6.2. The 95% confidence intervals are included.

TABLE 6.2   The determinants of turnout (Models 1–6)

	(Model 1)	(Model 2)	(Model 3)	(Model 4)	(Model 5)	(Model 6)
Age	2.15***	2.29***	1.73***	1.81***	1.73***	1.53***
	(0.13)	(0.14)	(0.17)	(0.17)	(0.17)	(0.17)
Post-secondary education		0.58***	0.41***	0.33***	0.36***	0.33***
		(0.05)	(0.05)	(0.06)	(0.06)	(0.06)
Political interest			2.28***	1.26***	0.74***	0.60***
			(0.12)	(0.14)	(0.15)	(0.16)
Duty				2.29***	1.96***	1.92***
				(0.07)	(0.06)	(0.06)
Care					1.50***	1.40***
					(0.19)	(0.18)
Ease						1.14***
						(0.18)
Constant	−0.43***	−0.58***	−1.85***	−2.24***	−2.72***	−3.29***
	(0.05)	(0.06)	(0.07)	(0.08)	(0.13)	(0.17)
Observations	26,105	26,105	26,105	26,105	26,105	26,105
Pseudo R^2	.056	.068	.124	.203	.217	.229

Notes: Entries are logistic regression coefficients. Robust standard errors, clustered by election, are in parentheses. Election fixed effects are included.
* $p < .05$, ** $p < .01$, *** $p < .001$

to maximum.[5] The most appropriate comparison, however, is between someone at .5 and someone at 1 on the scale, that is, one standard deviation below and above the mean; in that case, the increase in the propensity to vote is 14 percentage points.

This is far from being negligible, but the impact of ease of voting is clearly weaker than that of the previous three considerations, which is consistent with our motivational model. Obviously, people consider the cost of voting and many people would abstain if they expected to wait a full hour in line to cast a vote. The bottom line, however, is that for the great majority of people, the cost of voting is small. The turnout decision boils down to whether the person is sufficiently motivated to take a little time to cast a vote.

7

Is Voting a Habit?

There is strong stability in individuals' propensity to vote over time. If someone votes in a given election, she is likely to vote in subsequent elections (Miller and Shanks 1996; Blais 2000). There are two interpretations for this stability. The first is that the decision to vote or abstain is mostly shaped by deep attitudes, such as political interest and sense of civic duty, that are stable over the life cycle. Those who like politics and who feel that they have a moral obligation to vote maintain their political interest and sense of duty over time, and consequently keep voting, while those who are not interested in politics and have no sense of duty keep abstaining because they have no reason to vote. In other words, people keep making the same choices because they maintain the same attitudes over time. This is the interpretation that is consistent with the theoretical argumentation and the empirical evidence that we have presented in the previous chapters.

The alternative interpretation is that after some time, people develop a habit of voting or abstaining, and they subsequently vote or abstain simply because they have been voting or abstaining in the past. They repeat the same behaviour because this is what they are used to doing. Voting or abstaining becomes a habit.

The first question to ask is: What is a habit? Unfortunately, most of the authors who put forward the habit interpretation do not take the time to clarify what habit means or implies. We start with the conventional definition, which we take from Dictionary.com: it is "an acquired behavior pattern regularly followed until it has become almost involuntary."[1] We will conclude that a voting habit exists if the behaviour (voting or abstaining) is repeated (there is a pattern) on a regular basis and it is at least partly automatic.

The first criterion (repeated) is the easiest to observe. There are clearly some people who vote or abstain almost or all the time. This is not sufficient, however. As mentioned above, someone might vote all the time because she feels it is her duty to vote. It would be inappropriate to label that person a habitual voter in the same way that it would be incorrect to say that the junior co-author, who loves going to a karaoke every Friday night, is a habitual "karaokeer." A habit entails more than repeated behaviour.

The second criterion is regularity. In some sense, there is regularity in elections, as the presence of regular elections is one of the necessary conditions of an electoral democracy (Powell 1982, 3). As pointed out in Chapter 1, the modern citizen is invited to go to the polls on average once a year. But this does not mean that voting is regular. There may be an election every year but there are different types of elections – national, subnational, and supranational; legislative or executive – elections, primaries, and referenda. These various types of elections are often held under different rules and at different times of the year. In fact, there is greater regularity in other domains. Compare the regularity of elections with that of the Roland Garros tennis tournament, the Grammy Awards ceremony, or the Eurovision contest. Furthermore, as far as we can tell, there is little evidence that many voters vote in all types of elections. In short, elections do not appear to be very regular, and there are thus good reasons to be skeptical about the existence of a voting habit.

The final criterion for the existence of a habit is its automatic (involuntary) character. We would not say that a person who loves fishing and regularly goes fishing has the habit of fishing. The fishing activity must be at least partly automatic, that is, partly independent of her inner motivations. Perhaps she does not love fishing as much as she used to, but she keeps on because this is what she is used to doing. The habitual voter keeps on voting because this is what she has done in the past, at least in part independently of her present motivations. If we contrast "habitual" and "non-habitual" citizens, we would expect the former group's decision to be less strongly affected by present considerations.

With these clarifications in mind, let us review previous work on voting as a habit.

Eric Plutzer (2002) was the first author to systematize the habitual voter model.[2] Plutzer makes an important distinction between persistence and inertia. Both lead to stable behaviour. There is persistence when the causes of stability reside in factors that "occurred many years earlier," such as interest and duty, while there is inertia when "the roots of current turnout can be found in voting behavior in the previous one or two elections" (42). In a nutshell, habit corresponds to inertia, whereby the decision to vote in a specific election depends on the decision made previously rather than on the attitudes or factors that shaped the initial decision. This is fully consistent with the distinction that we have made. Habit entails at least some degree of automaticity, such that those who repeat their behaviour do so at least partly independently of inner motivations. Plutzer notes that there is both habitual voting and habitual abstention, though he adds that the latter tends to be weaker than the former.

Plutzer uses M. Kent Jennings and Richard G. Niemi's three-wave Youth-Parent Socialization Panel Study (Niemi and Jennings 1991; Jennings, Markus, and Niemi 1991), which enables him to examine the factors that affect the decision to vote or abstain in the 1968, 1972, 1976, and 1980 US elections among those who became eligible to vote for the first time in 1968. He examines the impact of four blocks of variables (demographic and parental characteristics; youth factors in 1965; factors occurring between 1965 and 1968; and factors occurring after 1968).

This is a rich and fascinating study, which shows that different factors are at play for the first and later elections. It is not clear at all, however, what this tells us about voting as a habit. Plutzer proposes a developmental theory that assumes that most citizens are habitual voters or abstainers, but he does not clearly identify which specific predictions follow from the habit hypothesis. He seems to believe that the data show inertia because "parental resources continue to distinguish voters from non-voters in succeeding elections" (Plutzer 2002, 54). But another interpretation is that parental resources remain significant in later elections precisely because they shape political interest and civic duty, which affect the propensity to vote in every election. Furthermore, the most striking finding in Plutzer's final model (table 7) is that whether the respondent's parents voted in the previous (1964) election is the sole parental variable (among five, the others being parental political interest, political knowledge, political trust, and strength of partisanship) that is significantly correlated with voting in the first election, and that this variable is not associated with turnout in subsequent elections. Plutzer's research provides useful insight into the many factors that affect turnout in young adulthood, but he fails to provide clear evidence of habit.

Habit is also central to Mark Franklin's seminal study (2004) of voter turnout. Franklin argues that over-time variations in voter turnout are shaped by the dynamics of electoral competition. He adds that this is so only for those who have not acquired the habit of voting. There is a strong inertia component among "old" cohorts, and therefore the impact of electoral competition should be strongest among "new" cohorts. New cohorts are defined as those facing their first three elections, which corresponds to those aged 18 to 27 in a given election.[3] The prediction is thus an interaction effect between competition and the new-cohort variable.

Franklin tests his predictions with both aggregate and individual-level data. At the aggregate level, Franklin examines turnout in national elections in twenty-two countries between 1945 and 2000, and shows that interactive variables corresponding to the combination of "competition" variables such as margin of victory and the proportion of the electorate that corresponds to a new cohort are highly significant. At the individual level, he examines post-election surveys conducted in Germany to demonstrate that variables corresponding to the interaction of majority status or margin of victory and whether the person is a member of the new cohort are strongly significant, even after controlling for a host of other variables.

Franklin's approach, which consists of testing the habit hypothesis through an interaction effect with age, is original and compelling. If there is a "automatic" voting habit that is acquired over time, the new cohorts, who do not yet have a habit, should respond to the short-term dynamics of electoral competition, while the old cohorts should continue to vote or abstain as they have done in the past, independently of the particular context of an election. The basic idea, which is that those with a habit should be more or less impervious to new contextual factors, and that the habit should be strongly correlated with age, as it takes time to develop, makes a lot of sense.

Franklin does not systematically test the presence of interaction effects in his empirical analyses, however. More precisely, as demonstrated by Thomas Brambor, William Clark, and Matt Golder (2006), the only way to appropriately test interaction models is to include both main and interaction effects. Franklin fails to include main effects, and his data therefore do not allow us to conclude, as the voting habit model would predict, that old cohorts are less affected by short-term factors such as the competitiveness of the election.

André Blais and Daniel Rubenson (2013) perform an analysis along the lines proposed by Franklin; they test for an interaction effect between contextual variables such as margin of victory and whether one belongs to a new cohort – that is, the election at hand is the first, second, or third in which voters are eligible to vote. The prediction, inspired by Franklin, is that members of the new cohort will be more inclined to vote when the election is closely contested (small margin), whereas members of older cohorts will not be affected, as they vote or abstain out of inertia (habit).

Blais and Rubenson (2013) test this prediction with survey data from eighty-three elections in eight countries, and they find that contextual variables such as margin of victory (at the national level) do *not* have a stronger effect among new cohorts. They repeat the same analysis with nine elections held in Britain between 1974 and 2005, and this time they consider margin of victory in the local district.

Again, they find no significant interaction effect between (local) margin of victory and being a member of a new cohort. These findings are inconsistent with the voting habit interpretation.

Blais and Rubenson (2013) provide additional support for the view that the over-time stability in turnout is due to the presence of strong and stable attitudes such as political interest and sense of civic duty, rather than simple inertia (habit). They analyze the 1952–92 American National Election Studies (ANES) dataset and show that indeed more recent cohorts (the post-boomers) are less inclined to vote, but that this can be fully explained by their attitudes (weaker sense of duty and lower external efficacy). They also use the 1956–60 and 1972–76 panel surveys and find that sense of civic duty measured four years earlier successfully predicts the propensity to vote four years later, even controlling for turnout in the previous election.

Another interesting study from this perspective is that of Edward Fieldhouse and David Cutts (2012). They examine turnout in the 2001 British election and focus on newly registered first-time electors (NRFTE) who come of age during the year of the election. They find that these "attainers" are less likely to vote, but, more importantly, that the impact of living with other voters is stronger for these electors. This could be because they have not yet acquired the habit of voting and are therefore more strongly influenced by their environment. But that interpretation is problematic once we consider the fact that this interaction effect does not emerge for those aged 19 and 20 (see table 4 in Fieldhouse and Cutts 2012), and for whom this was also the first election in which they had the right to vote. A more plausible interpretation is that 18-year-old first-time electors are simply more likely to be affected by their parents' decision to vote or abstain. These findings, therefore, do not confirm the habit hypothesis.

John Aldrich, Jacob Montgomery, and Wendy Wood (2011) provide still another test. They define habitual voters as those who report that they have always voted in previous elections and who have been living in the same location for at least ten years. They estimate the impact of standard determinants of turnout (borrowed from Rosenstone and Hansen 1993) among habitual and non-habitual voters, and predict that these determinants will have a stronger impact among non-habitual voters. There is much to be applauded in this approach. If voting is for some a habit, it should follow that attitudes, such as political interest and sense of duty, that drive the decision to vote or not to vote have little impact on them.

The authors examine the ANES surveys of 1964, 1972, 1976, and 1980 with validated vote. When they test the crucial hypothesis that motivations are less strongly related to the decision to vote or abstain among those with a strong habit, they focus on five "decision variables": care about the outcome, strength of party identification, internal efficacy, external efficacy, and contacted by a candidate. Their initial results (table 4 of Aldrich, Montgomery, and Wood 2011, columns 1 and 2) confirm that each of these five determinants has a weaker impact among those with a habit. The findings with the full model (including all control variables; see table 4, columns 7 and 8) are not so neat, however. While care, external efficacy, and contacted have larger effects in the no-habit group, the impact of internal efficacy and party identification is in fact larger in the habit group. These results are ambiguous, and we conclude that the key hypothesis that those with a habit are less influenced by motivational variables is not supported.

Other scholars have tackled the question of voting as a habit using experimental designs. Alan Gerber, Donald Green, and Ron Shachar (2003, 541) report the results of a large-scale field experiment run in 1998 with more than 25,000 observations from the city of New Haven, Connecticut. The treatments were to receive a message to vote through either direct mail or canvassing, while the control group received no treatment. Canvassing did increase voter turnout in 1998 but, more importantly, it also had an impact in the 1999 "uneventful reelection of a Democratic incumbent in a city where Democrats hold a large majority of party registrants" (545), even controlling for the 1996 participation.[4] These results were replicated in several additional experiments (Gerber, Green, and Larimer 2008; Sinclair, McConnell, and Green 2012; Coppock and Green 2017).

David Cutts, Edward Fieldhouse, and Peter John (2009) also used experimental data during the 2005 UK general election, which used a treatment to boost electoral participation by using telephone or door-to-door canvassing. The authors acknowledge that the effects were small, but they claim that the habit-forming impact was "large" because the probability of having voted in 2005 increased by half the probability of having voted in the 2006 local election. Their approach is summed up thus: "By artificially stimulating voting in one election we are able to gauge the effect of habit by observing whether there is any downstream increase in the propensity to vote in the experimental treatment group" (242).

These studies show that the impact of get-out-the-vote experiments is not purely temporary – in other words, those who are convinced to vote in an election are more likely to vote in subsequent elections. This research cannot tell us, however, *why* the impact persists. It could be that some people take on the habit of voting, but, as pointed out by Plutzer (2002), the presence of persistence does not entail the presence of inertia (or habit). The treatments may have enhanced people's level of interest in politics, their sense of civic duty, or their perception of how easy or difficult it is to vote.[5] To demonstrate that habit is the causal mechanism, researchers would need to show that the persistent impact is not due to the treatment's effect on the basic motivations (such as political interest or civic duty) that drive the decision to vote or abstain.

Kevin Denny and Orla Doyle (2009) use panel data to investigate the habit hypothesis. They argue that most studies on turnout as a habit use cross-sectional data and that their panel data can control for fixed individual characteristics to isolate the impact of habit. More specifically, their dynamic model of voter turnout controls for two forms of unobserved heterogeneity: fixed effects and initial conditions. They use the British National Child Development study, which tracks respondents from birth to middle age. They examine three waves (when respondents were 23, 33, and 41–42), which enables them to analyze turnout in three elections (1979, 1987, and 1997). They control for several fixed characteristics and isolate the impact of voting in the previous election, which proves to be significant. They conclude that voting in an election increases by 13 percentage points the probability of voting in the next election.

Such an analysis is compelling only to the extent to which voting stability cannot be explained by omitted variables such as political interest and sense of civic duty. As the authors acknowledge, "omitting such explanatory factors from the model may introduce bias into the parameter estimates ... It is critical to control for such fixed effects unobserved heterogeneity as failing to do so will result in an over-estimation of the degree of persistence in voter turnout" (Denny and Doyle 2009, 20). Their model does include controls for socio-demographic characteristics, physical and mental health, personality traits, and cognitive ability, but does not incorporate crucial motivational attitudes such as general interest in politics and the sense of duty to vote. Thus, we cannot dismiss the possibility that the observed effect of having voted in previous elections merely reflects the impact of these unobserved attitudes.

Elias Dinas (2012) also relies on panel data to examine the formation of voting habits. The data come from the four waves of the youth sample of the Socialization Panel Study (Jennings et al. 2005). The participants were born in 1947 or 1948 and were approximately 18 years old in 1965 (first wave of the study) and about 21 at the time of the 1968 US presidential election. Dinas compares the propensity to vote in 1970 among those who were not eligible to vote in 1968, among those who were eligible and did vote, and among those who were eligible but did not vote. He estimates that the likelihood of voting in 1970 was 12 percentage points higher among those who were eligible to vote, and that having voted in 1968 increased the probability of voting in 1970 by 27 points. This is interpreted as evidence that voting is habit forming.

The limitations of this study are the same as those of Denny and Doyle's study (2009). The analysis does not include as control variables basic attitudes such as political interest and sense of civic duty, which we have shown to be crucial.[6] Again, an alternative interpretation is that the relationship is spurious, as the "real" causal factors are the motivations that did (or did not) drive people to the polls in the previous election. We should also mention that the estimated impact of previous voting appears to be implausibly high.

Another related approach is that of Marc Meredith (2009), who shows, through a regression discontinuity design, that California voters who were just eligible to vote in 2000 were more likely to vote in 2004 than those who were just a few weeks younger and were not eligible in 2000. As Meredith correctly points out, this demonstrates the presence of persistence in electoral participation. In this case, this means that past eligibility affects subsequent turnout; the mere fact of having the opportunity to vote in an election makes one more likely to vote in the subsequent election. One plausible interpretation of such finding is that this is because some people form the habit of voting. This is not impossible, though it is a bit odd that the habit is acquired so quickly. An alternative interpretation is that voting a second time is easier than voting for the first time, like playing chess. Having voted once lowers the perceived cost of voting, in the absence of any habit.

Furthermore, Meredith's finding that past eligibility positively affects subsequent turnout has not been replicated in subsequent research. John Holbein and Sunshine Hillygus (2016) examined Florida's voter files for the 2012 election and found, through a regression discontinuity design, that those who were marginally eligible to vote in 2008 were actually less likely to vote than those who were marginally ineligible. The result is exactly the opposite of that reported by Meredith. In a subsequent study, Brendan Nyhan, Christopher Skovron, and Rocio Titiunik (2017) show that these findings are highly sensitive to differential registration bias.

All these eligibility studies were conducted in the United States. Is there a similar pattern in Europe? Johannes Bergh (2013) examines the impact of a "natural" experiment in which the voting age was lowered from 18 to 16 in a group of Norwegian municipalities, and seeks to determine whether the 16- and 17-year-olds in these municipalities have a higher level of turnout in the subsequent 2013 parliamentary election than the 16- and 17-year-olds in municipalities where the voting age had not been lowered and who were therefore ineligible to vote in the 2011 local elections. The results are surprising: turnout was in fact 5 percentage points lower in the treatment group. There is no evidence of habit here.

Still another approach is to examine whether unanticipated exceptional increase or decrease in turnout in one election leads to a permanent increase or decrease in turnout in subsequent elections. Such evidence is provided by Thomas Fujiwara, Kyle Meng, and Tom Vogl (2016), who examine county-level data on US presidential elections held from 1952 to 2012 and find that rainfall on election day reduces turnout not only in that election but also in the subsequent election. It should be pointed out, however, that no such pattern emerges for mid-term elections. Furthermore, when it comes to explaining these results, the authors conclude that "the consumption value of voting, stemming from civic duty, ethics, or social pressure ... is perhaps the most plausible mechanism" (184). We fail to see how civic duty can be equated with habit.

In the same vein, Michael Bechtel, Dominik Hangartner, and Lukas Schmid (2018) test the proposition that compulsory voting makes people develop the habit of voting, such that turnout remains high even after the abolition of compulsory voting. They compare the evolution of turnout in federal referenda in the canton of Vaud, Switzerland, before and after the introduction of compulsory voting in that canton in 1924 as well as after its abolition in 1948, and in the cantons without compulsory voting. They find that compulsory voting increased turnout by 30 percentage points but that the effect vanished immediately after its abolition: "When Vaud abolished compulsory voting, the treatment effect drops to 0 ... this thorough law enforcement did not lead individuals to develop a voting habit" (472).

To say the least, the empirical evidence about the habit hypothesis is ambiguous. Some studies provide some support but as many simply disconfirm it. Furthermore, even those studies whose findings are consistent with the habit hypothesis can be interpreted differently. While we do not find these studies to be entirely compelling, they suggest a fruitful approach for testing the habit hypothesis. We draw two main conclusions from this review of prior research. First, habit should be strongly correlated with age (Franklin 2004). A habit develops over time, and so older citizens are much more likely to be habituated. The exact form of that relationship is not clear, but age appears to be an appropriate proxy for the propensity to have a habit. In fact, a recent study by Jean-Yves Dormagen and Laura Michel (2017) shows a strong correlation between age and constant voting/abstention in the two rounds of the 2002, 2007, and 2012 French presidential and legislative elections.[7] Second, the habit interpretation predicts interaction effects: we expect citizens with a habit to be less strongly influenced by present contextual factors or attitudinal motivations than those with no habit, since they are simply repeating what they have done in the past.

If many people form a habit of voting or abstaining, it should follow that the basic considerations that shape the decision to vote or not to vote progressively come to have weaker effects as individuals repeat the decisions made in prior elections regardless of whether these considerations change over time. The most straightforward prediction is that the four considerations that we have examined in the previous chapters have a weaker impact among older citizens.

Table 7.1 (Model 1) tests this prediction with data from the Making Electoral Democracy Work (MEDW) project, which entails a negative interaction between each consideration and age. The prediction is disconfirmed. Only one coefficient for the interaction terms is significant, and three of them even have the wrong positive sign. This analysis assumes a linear relationship between age and habit: the older you are, the stronger your habit. Franklin (2004) argues that most people have formed a habit after ten years. In Model 2 of Table 7.1, we dichotomize age into a new and old (aged 28 and above) cohort. It turns out that none of the interactive terms is significant, and again three coefficients have the wrong positive sign. In Model 3, we use another definition, according to which the old cohort is aged over 35, and we can see that the only significant interaction is in the wrong direction.

In short, there are only two interaction effects between our four basic considerations and age or cohort, and one of the two is positive, contrary to what the habit model would predict. These findings clearly disconfirm the habit interpretation. Contrary to the habit hypothesis,

TABLE 7.1 Interactions between age and considerations (MEDW)

	(Model 1) Age = continuous	(Model 2) Age > 28 years	(Model 3) Age > 35 years
Age	1.03**	0.57**	0.32
	(0.40)	(0.18)	(0.17)
Post-secondary education	0.33***	0.27***	0.32***
	(0.06)	(0.06)	(0.06)
Political interest	1.07***	1.06***	0.84***
	(0.31)	(0.26)	(0.23)
Duty	1.65***	1.89***	1.73***
	(0.15)	(0.18)	(0.10)
Care	1.22***	1.29***	1.26***
	(0.23)	(0.30)	(0.20)
Ease of voting	0.89***	1.17***	1.03***
	(0.21)	(0.25)	(0.22)
Age × political interest	−1.20*	−0.39	−0.25
	(0.52)	(0.25)	(0.16)
Age × duty	0.68	0.02	0.28*
	(0.39)	(0.22)	(0.14)
Age × care	0.45	0.16	0.23
	(0.61)	(0.35)	(0.30)
Age × ease of voting	0.65	0.04	0.18
	(0.40)	(0.23)	(0.18)
Constant	−3.17***	−3.37***	−3.05***
	(0.20)	(0.21)	(0.17)
Observations	26,105	26,105	26,105
Pseudo R^2	.230	.223	.229

Notes: Entries are logistic regression coefficients. Robust standard errors, clustered by election, are in parentheses. Election fixed effects are included.
* $p < .05$, ** $p < .01$, *** $p < .001$

interest, duty, care, and ease do *not* have a weaker impact on the turnout decision of older respondents, who have presumably acquired the habit of voting or abstaining. Age is of course only a proxy for habit, but it is, we would argue, a good proxy, since the likelihood of having acquired a habit should be directly correlated with age. Furthermore, this is the very proxy that has been utilized by Franklin (2004), the most prominent author to have put forward the habit interpretation. Our results challenge the view that people keep on making the same decision to vote or abstain, regardless of their interest in politics or their sense of civic duty.

We perform a similar analysis using the most recent module of the Comparative Study of Electoral System (CSES). We examine the interaction of two major correlates of voter turnout – political knowledge and party identification – with age.[8] In most countries, there were four indicators of political knowledge (with the exception of Ireland 2011 and Canada 2011, where there were only one and two items, respectively). Respondents had to correctly identify the person responsible for the finance portfolio, the unemployment rate in the country, the secretary-general of the United Nations, and the party that placed second in the election. The mean knowledge score is .41. For party identification, if the respondent says that she does not feel close to a political party, she is coded 0. If she feels close to a political party but "not really close," she is coded .33. If she is "somewhat close" she is coded .67, and if she is "really close" she is coded 1. The mean score is .34. The dependent variable is self-reported vote; 83% of respondents claim to have voted.

We use the same three ways of operationalizing age as in the analysis reported in Table 7.1. As shown in Table 7.2, none of the interactions is significant – even with an impressively high number of observations – and four out of six coefficients are in the wrong direction. All in all, we find no support for the habitual voter model when we use age as a proxy for habit. Even if age is, as we believe, a good proxy for habit, it remains, of course, an indirect indicator. Would it be possible to test the habit hypothesis with a more direct indicator?

To test another operationalization of habit, we use the American National Election Study (ANES). We select the 1972, 1976, and 1980 elections, which include indicators of interest, duty, and care. The dependent variable is self-reported turnout, which is between 71% and 73% in these three elections. Our independent variables are political interest, caring about the outcome, duty to vote, and strength of party

TABLE 7.2 Interactions between age and considerations (CSES)

	(Model 1) Age = continuous	(Model 2) Age > 28 years	(Model 3) Age > 35 years
Age	1.66***	0.62***	0.64***
	(0.26)	(0.11)	(0.09)
Woman	0.12**	0.13**	0.13**
	(0.04)	(0.04)	(0.04)
Education	0.49***	0.38***	0.44***
	(0.07)	(0.07)	(0.08)
Political information	1.54***	1.60***	1.55***
	(0.17)	(0.20)	(0.19)
PID (party identification)	1.82***	1.78***	1.83***
	(0.13)	(0.13)	(0.14)
Age × political information	0.05	0.01	0.04
	(0.43)	(0.13)	(0.16)
Age × PID	−0.17	0.03	−0.05
	(0.28)	(0.15)	(0.12)
Constant	0.35***	0.38**	0.46***
	(0.11)	(0.13)	(0.11)
Observations	34,037	34,037	34,037
Pseudo R^2	.178	.171	.174

Notes: Entries are logistic regression coefficients. Robust standard errors, clustered by election, are in parentheses. Election fixed effects are included.
* $p < .05$, ** $p < .01$, *** $p < .001$

identification, plus age, gender, and education. An advantage of this dataset is that it enables us to stay close to our model, as three of our four main variables are included. The only difference is that ease of voting is not included and is replaced with party identification, which is a crucial dimension in the American context (Lewis-Beck et al. 2008).

Respondents were asked about their interest in the current campaign: "Some people don't pay much attention to the political campaigns. How about you, would you say that you have been very much interested, somewhat interested, or not much interested in following the political campaigns so far this year?" The response categories are coded 1, .5, and 0, respectively. The mean is .51 for the 1972 and 1980 elections and .58 in 1976. The care question is: "Generally speaking, would you say that you personally care a good deal which party wins the presidential election this fall, or don't you care very much which party wins?" The voter is coded 1 if she cares a great deal and 0 otherwise. The mean ranges from .54 to .60 in the three elections.

The questions used for strength of partisanship are the following: "Generally speaking, do you usually think of yourself as a Republican, a Democrat, and Independent, or what?" (If Republican or Democrat) "Would you call yourself a strong Republican/Democrat or not very strong?" (If Independent, other, or no preference) "Do you think of yourself as closer to the Republican or Democratic party?" Respondents are coded 0 if they are independent or apolitical, .33 if they are independent leaning towards a party, .67 if they are a weak partisan, and 1 if they are a strong partisan. The mean is .58 in each election. The duty question asks respondents whether they think that a person should vote if she doesn't care how an election comes out. It is coded 1 if the respondent thinks that she should vote and 0 otherwise. The mean is about .54 in all three elections. Finally, we add as control variables age (rescaled 0 to 1), gender (male being the reference category), and education (coded 1 for 12th grade completed and 0 if not).

We examine the interaction of these attitudes with an indicator of habit, which is measured by the consistency of voting or abstaining in previous elections. The ANES data allow us to operationalize habit in a different way. The question is as follows: "In the elections for President since you have been old enough to vote, would you say you have voted in all of them, most of them, some of them or none of them?" We test two ways of operationalizing habit. First, only those who answer "always" (about 50% of the sample) are considered to have a habit and are thus coded 1. Second, we also code 1 those who answer "none of them" (about 10%) as habitual (abstainers).[9]

Table 7.3 presents the results. We see that each of the motivational variables has a strong and significant impact on the propensity to vote. We also see that habit has a significant main effect when only those

TABLE 7.3   The interaction between habit and motivational variables (ANES)

	(Model 1) 1972	(Model 2) 1972	(Model 3) 1976	(Model 4) 1976	(Model 5) 1980	(Model 6) 1980
Consistency =	Always	Always or never	Always	Always or never	Always	Always or never
Age	−0.20	0.26	0.71*	0.83**	0.84**	1.09***
	(0.27)	(0.26)	(0.29)	(0.28)	(0.27)	(0.26)
Woman	−0.19	−0.22*	−0.42***	−0.45***	−0.13	−0.10
	(0.11)	(0.11)	(0.13)	(0.12)	(0.12)	(0.12)
Education	0.69***	0.82***	0.75***	0.93***	0.29*	0.47***
	(0.13)	(0.12)	(0.15)	(0.15)	(0.13)	(0.13)
Political interest	1.02***	1.08***	0.81***	0.68**	0.99***	0.80***
	(0.18)	(0.20)	(0.20)	(0.23)	(0.21)	(0.23)
Consistency	2.20***	−0.01	2.31***	−0.28	2.06***	−0.01
	(0.39)	(0.25)	(0.40)	(0.26)	(0.35)	(0.29)
PID (party identification)	0.84***	0.61**	0.81***	0.66**	1.36***	0.89***
	(0.20)	(0.23)	(0.21)	(0.25)	(0.24)	(0.27)
Care	0.53*	0.64***	0.47	0.36	0.24	0.10
	(0.26)	(0.17)	(0.34)	(0.19)	(0.21)	(0.17)
Civic duty	0.54*	0.96***	0.35	1.03***	0.25	0.42*
	(0.25)	(0.16)	(0.30)	(0.18)	(0.21)	(0.17)
Consistency × political interest	−0.49	−0.02	−0.24	0.84*	−0.24	0.58
	(0.42)	(0.31)	(0.49)	(0.35)	(0.36)	(0.34)
Consistency × PID	−0.05	0.92**	0.04	0.46	−1.66***	−0.04
	(0.46)	(0.33)	(0.46)	(0.36)	(0.43)	(0.37)
Consistency × care	−0.12	−0.21	−0.10	−0.02	−0.32	−0.15
	(0.29)	(0.22)	(0.37)	(0.25)	(0.27)	(0.25)
Consistency × duty	0.04	−0.48*	0.36	−0.45	−0.11	−0.22
	(0.28)	(0.21)	(0.33)	(0.23)	(0.26)	(0.24)
Constant	−1.17***	−1.00***	−1.17***	−0.75***	−1.86***	−1.52***
	(0.17)	(0.20)	(0.18)	(0.21)	(0.20)	(0.23)
Observations	2,269	2,269	1,898	1,898	1,406	1,406
Pseudo R^2	.242	.175	.247	.169	.147	.105

Notes: Entries are logistic regression coefficients. Robust standard errors are in parentheses.
* $p < .05$, ** $p < .01$, *** $p < .001$

who say that they always vote are construed as habitual. This main effect is misleading, however, as it also picks up the impact of all the other attitudes that affect the likelihood of always voting and that have not been included in our model. As both Franklin (2004) and Aldrich, Montgomery, and Wood (2011) have argued, the crucial test of the habit hypothesis is whether the factors that drive the decision to vote have a weaker impact among those who are construed to be habitual. The habit interpretation predicts negative interactions between habit and interest, duty, care, and party identification.

Table 7.3 shows that this prediction is not borne out. Among the twenty-four interaction terms included in Table 7.3, twenty are *not* statistically significant. Among the four significant interactions, two have the wrong (positive) sign.

Aldrich, Montgomery, and Wood (2011) argue that having a habit entails not only repeating the same behaviour over time but also doing so in a similar context. They consider that one cannot have developed a habit if she has not experienced a stable context long enough. They thus introduce a second condition for someone to be construed as "habitual": the person must have lived in the same location for at least ten years. Are the patterns similar if we add this second condition? Table 7.4 presents the findings. We can see that the results are very similar. Only one of the twenty-four interaction effects is significant and negative.

The dependent variable in all these analyses is self-reported turnout. As a robustness check, we replicated the analysis using validated vote for the 1980 American election – the only election that has a validated vote for the entire sample. Table A.5 of Appendix 2 displays the results. Only one negative interaction reaches statistical significance (out of eight interaction coefficients) and almost half of the effects are in the wrong direction. All in all, there is no coherent pattern and the main conclusion remains the same as for our analyses based on self-reported turnout.

It is now part of the conventional wisdom that voting is a habit. That conventional wisdom needs to be challenged. Much depends, of

TABLE 7.4 The interaction between habit (including having lived in the same location for at least 10 years) and motivational variables (ANES)

	(Model 1) 1972	(Model 2) 1972	(Model 3) 1976	(Model 4) 1976	(Model 5) 1980	(Model 6) 1980
Consistency =	Always	Always or never	Always	Always or never	Always	Always or never
Age	−0.26	0.06	0.22	0.46	0.71**	0.93***
	(0.27)	(0.26)	(0.29)	(0.29)	(0.26)	(0.26)
Woman	−0.16	−0.19	−0.43***	−0.46***	−0.08	−0.09
	(0.11)	(0.11)	(0.12)	(0.12)	(0.12)	(0.12)
Education	0.89***	0.90***	1.05***	1.04***	0.46***	0.54***
	(0.13)	(0.12)	(0.15)	(0.14)	(0.13)	(0.13)
Political interest	1.12***	1.13***	0.95***	0.97***	1.05***	0.90***
	(0.17)	(0.18)	(0.18)	(0.18)	(0.19)	(0.20)
Consistency	2.83***	0.34	1.92*	−0.16	2.13***	0.13
	(0.51)	(0.28)	(0.88)	(0.40)	(0.43)	(0.31)
PID (party identification)	0.86***	0.77***	0.83***	0.83***	0.97***	0.80***
	(0.19)	(0.20)	(0.19)	(0.19)	(0.21)	(0.22)
Care	0.52	0.62**	0.85	0.32	−0.10	−0.08
	(0.32)	(0.21)	(0.80)	(0.39)	(0.29)	(0.23)
Civic duty	0.14	0.97***	1.98*	2.30***	0.13	0.39
	(0.32)	(0.21)	(0.84)	(0.40)	(0.29)	(0.23)
Consistency × political interest	−0.56	−0.03	0.69	0.76	−0.32	0.67
	(0.49)	(0.35)	(0.86)	(0.56)	(0.43)	(0.37)
Consistency × PID	−0.44	0.67	−0.49	0.23	−1.00	0.15
	(0.57)	(0.36)	(1.23)	(0.63)	(0.51)	(0.41)
Consistency × care	−0.04	−0.13	−0.51	0.03	0.18	0.14
	(0.34)	(0.25)	(0.81)	(0.41)	(0.32)	(0.27)
Consistency × duty	0.56	−0.37	−1.28	−1.70***	0.13	−0.12
	(0.34)	(0.24)	(0.85)	(0.42)	(0.32)	(0.27)
Constant	−1.21***	−1.09***	−0.83***	−0.77***	−1.67***	−1.52***
	(0.17)	(0.18)	(0.17)	(0.18)	(0.19)	(0.20)
Observations	2,269	2,269	1,898	1,898	1,406	1,406
Pseudo R^2	.223	.174	.208	.177	.129	.105

Notes: Entries are logistic regression coefficients. Robust standard errors are in parentheses.
* $p < .05$, ** $p < .01$, *** $p < .001$

course, on how one defines habit. If habit solely means stable, repeated behaviour, then of course there is a habitual component in voting. But as Plutzer (2002) points out, habit also entails inertia, the idea that people repeat the same behaviour just because they behaved a certain way in the past, independent of the motivations or factors that shaped their initial decisions.

We have argued, following Franklin (2004) and Aldrich, Montgomery, and Wood (2011), that the most appropriate way to test the habit hypothesis is to show that the motivations that shape the decision to vote or abstain have less leverage among those who are deemed to be habitual; there should be a negative interaction effect between motivational attitudes and habit. We tested that hypothesis with age as a proxy for the propensity to be habitual (as per Franklin 2004) or with a more direct indicator (whether the respondent says that she always votes or abstains, as per Aldrich, Montgomery, and Wood 2011), and with three different datasets: MEDW, CSES, and ANES. We systematically fail to observe the significantly negative interaction predicted by the habit model.

Many experimental studies have concluded that habitual voting is present on the basis of their finding that the impact of a given intervention is still felt at a subsequent election. Such a conclusion is unwarranted. What these studies show is that the impact of the intervention is not temporary, which is interesting. But these studies cannot tell us why the effect endures. It could be that some people acquired the habit, but it could also be that they acquired a new interest in politics or that they realized that voting is easier than they initially thought. If habit is to have any useful meaning, it needs to entail more than simple repeat – there has to be some element of inertia/automaticity. The best way to determine whether this is the case is to see, following Franklin (2004) and Aldrich, Montgomery, and Wood (2011), whether the factors that drive turnout have a weaker impact among those who are deemed to be habitual. As we have shown in this chapter, these empirical tests are conclusive: there is no support for the habit interpretation.

It is important to note that our empirical approach corresponds to the design that has been used by the two most important non-experimental studies that have supported the habit interpretation.[10] Following Franklin (2004), we have examined whether the factors that affect turnout have a weaker impact among older citizens (who have acquired a habit). Following Aldrich, Montgomery, and Wood (2011), we have determined whether motivations have a weaker effect among those who indicate that they have always voted or abstained. The empirical tests that we have performed are similar to those that have been presented by the proponents of the habit hypothesis. The basic idea is simple and intuitive. Those who are deemed to be habitual (older voters or those who say that they have always voted or abstained in the past) should be weakly affected by the context of the election or motivational variables. The idea has been proposed and implemented by researchers who argue that there is a voting habit. We have put that idea to systematic empirical test, and the data fail to support the hypothesis.

Clearly some people always vote, while others always abstain. Such stability should not be interpreted as evidence of habit. It makes more sense to interpret that stability as reflecting the fact that the decision to vote or abstain is shaped by deep attitudes such as political interest and sense of civic duty, attitudes that are stable over time and whose influence is felt election after election. We do not rule out the possibility that some people vote or abstain out of pure habit, but we are not convinced that it is necessary (or even useful) to include that dimension in a parsimonious model of turnout. Scholars who study vote choice, other forms of political participation, and the formation of public opinion have conducted their research without resorting to the habit concept. Scholars who study turnout should do the same.

8

Does It All Depend on the Context?

In this last chapter, we examine the broader implications of the framework proposed in this book. The emphasis has been on the motivations that shape individuals' decision to vote or not in an election. We have argued that the decision hinges on two general predispositions – how much one likes politics and whether one believes that she has a moral obligation to vote – and two more specific judgments – how much one cares about the outcome of the election and how easy or difficult it is to vote. We claim that with these four considerations we can make sense of most people's turnout decision most of the time, in a wide variety of contexts.[1]

We want to show that, together, these four considerations explain the turnout decision remarkably well. Until now, our goal has been to establish that each of these considerations has an independent impact on turnout. It is now time to appreciate their joint total effect. For this, we use the final regression in Table 6.2, Model 6, which includes the four considerations (plus age and education as controls). We can estimate the predicted probability of someone who is interested in politics, has a sense of duty, cares about the outcome, and finds voting easy versus someone who does not like politics, construes voting as a matter of personal choice, does not care much about the outcome, and does not perceive voting as being easy. As we have done in previous chapters, we can contrast people who are 1 standard deviation above and under the mean in each case, that is, those at .9 versus .3 on interest, those at .8 versus .0 on duty, and those at 1 versus .5 on both care and ease of voting.

The predicted probability of voting of someone who is low on each of these four considerations is 27%, while that of someone who is systematically high is 88%. Clearly these four considerations do not fully explain the turnout decision, but they matter *a lot*. There are, of course, election-specific factors at play as well. These election-specific factors are captured by the election dummies that are included in the model.

The bottom line, however, is that individual-level variables matter more than contextual ones. Following Miki Kittilson and Christopher Anderson (2011, 42), we can estimate how much variance in turnout is due to differences across individuals and differences across contexts (elections) through a multi-level modelization (i.e., mixed-effects logistic regression) that decomposes the variance between the two levels. It turns out that 94% of the variance is due to differences across individuals and 6% is due to macro-level factors. The emphasis that we have given to individual-level variables is thus fully justified.

We should note that contextual-level variables play a lesser role in our dataset than in Kittilson and Anderson's study (2011), where contextual factors account for 17% of the variance. The reason is that we have a more homogeneous set of elections. As explained in Chapter 1, we have decided to focus on elections in well-established countries where voting is not compulsory, with an overrepresentation of federal systems, and contextual variations are therefore smaller than in the Comparative Study of Electoral Systems (CSES) sample used by Kittilson and Anderson. But it is useful to keep in mind that even in the latter case, individual-level differences clearly trump contextual variations (83% versus 17%). And we have in our own dataset substantial contextual variation in culture, economic development, and political institutions.

These results confirm that context matters, that the same individual will be more (or less) likely to vote in certain types of elections or under certain circumstances, but also that the context is less crucial than individual motivations. At the end of the day, the decision to vote or abstain is a personal one, based on a combination of deep personal beliefs (political interest and sense of duty), judgments about what is at stake, and how easy and convenient the act of voting is.

It could be argued that the motivations that drive the decision to vote are themselves shaped by contextual factors. We acknowledge that this is at least partly the case with respect to care. Some elections are more salient than others and voters will care more about elections where the stakes are higher. But what is and is not salient is a subjective call, and those who happen to be interested in politics are prone to think that a lot is at stake in most elections while those who are not interested are inclined to be more skeptical. The consequence is that the former systematically care more about the outcome all the time.

There should be even less contextual variation with respect to the other variables. We do not have clear expectations about ease of voting. The rules that make it easier or more difficult to vote do vary across countries, but we do not see big differences except perhaps for Switzerland, where people can vote by mail. There may also be peculiar circumstances (heavy rain, illness) that make it more difficult for a person to vote in a specific election, but this should be exceptional.

We anticipate little contextual variation in levels of political interest and duty. Markus Prior (2019) shows that overall levels of political interest are remarkably stable over time. We see no particular reason why people would be more (or less) interested in politics in a specific country or region, except under exceptional circumstances.

The same pattern should apply to duty. We see no clear reason why the norm that there is a duty to vote would be stronger or weaker in some places.[2] David Campbell (2006) has argued that political homogeneity in the United States contributes to stronger civic norms, but he finds no correlation with religious or racial homogeneity, and it is not clear that this can be generalized outside the United States, as the evidence about the relationship between income or ethnic homogeneity and turnout is ambiguous (Cancela and Geys 2016, table 1).

There is the possibility that people feel less of a duty to vote in elections that they deem to be less important, and this may be why sense of duty is weaker in European elections (see Figure 4.1). But note

TABLE 8.1 Decomposition of the variance in political interest, sense of duty, care, and ease of voting using mixed-effects (multi-level) modelling

	(Model 1) Interest b/se	(Model 2) Duty b/se	(Model 3) Care b/se	(Model 4) Ease b/se
Fixed effects				
Constant	0.62***	0.48***	0.69***	0.71***
	(0.01)	(0.02)	(0.02)	(0.01)
Variance components				
Election-level	0.0006***	0.006***	0.005***	0.002***
	(0.0001)	(0.001)	(0.001)	(0.0007)
Individual-level	0.07***	0.13***	0.07***	0.08***
	(0.001)	(0.002)	(0.002)	(0.003)
ICC	0.8	4.5	7.5	3.1
N	26,105	26,105	26,105	26,105

Notes: Entries are OLS regression coefficients. Robust standard errors are in parentheses.
* $p < .05$, ** $p < .01$, *** $p < .001$

that duty is only slightly weaker in European elections, and the most remarkable fact is that duty varies remarkably little across types of election within a country (Galais and Blais 2016b).

In short, we believe that people's motivations to vote are driven by individual-level factors and that contextual variables play only a little part, particularly with respect to political interest and duty. Table 8.1 allows us to test these expectations. As we did for turnout, we perform a mixed-effects logistic regression to decompose the variance in political interest, duty, care, and ease due to differences across individuals and to differences across elections. The results are crystal-clear. Macro differences account for only 1% of the variance in interest, 3% in ease, 4% in duty, and 8% in care. As anticipated, contextual factors play a bigger role with respect to care, but the bottom line is that motivations depend fundamentally on individual-level factors.

The findings reported in this study are based on an additive model that allows us to estimate the independent impact of the four considerations and election-specific features captured by the series of election dummies. It could be argued that individual and contextual factors are not independent of each other – that is, individual considerations matter differently in different contexts. According to this view, we should be looking for contingent effects, whereby "the political context interacts with individuals' attitudes to affect their electoral behavior" (Dalton and Anderson 2011, 245).

Our point is not that there is no such contingent effect. It would be most surprising, indeed, if the relationship between political interest or civic duty and turnout were the same in all contexts. We contend, however, that contingent effects are infrequent and small.

Perhaps the most direct test of the contingent effect hypothesis is to re-estimate our model separately for each of the twenty-four elections. In each country, we ascertain the impact of each of the four considerations (political interest, duty, care, and ease) on the decision to vote or not. As previously, we control for age and education when analyzing the effect of interest; we also control for interest when looking at the impact of duty; we control for both duty and interest when sorting out the effect of care; and we include all three other considerations (plus age and education) when measuring the effect of ease. This yields a total of ninety-six coefficients, twenty-four for each of the four considerations.

The results of these estimations are summarized in Figure 8.1. We can see that ninety-five of the ninety-six coefficients have the expected positive sign, and that they are statistically significant in eighty-one cases. The magnitude of the coefficients does vary across elections, but we should not lose sight of the dominant pattern. In every election, each of these considerations matters. The same finding is reported by Anderson and Dalton (2011, 243): "The basic predictors of individual behavior work in the same direction even across the wide range of democracies."

The final analysis to be undertaken is to explicitly test for interaction effects between the four considerations and institutional rules. We focus on two institutional rules: electoral system and level of government. With respect to the electoral system, we distinguish

FIGURE 8.1 The impact of political interest, duty, care, and ease of voting in 24 elections

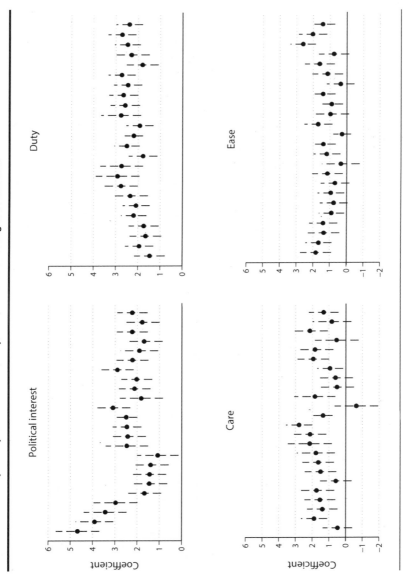

Notes: Coefficients are based on 24 separate logistic regressions for each variable. Dashed lines represent 95% confidence intervals.

FIGURE 8.2 The motivation to vote in PR and non-PR elections

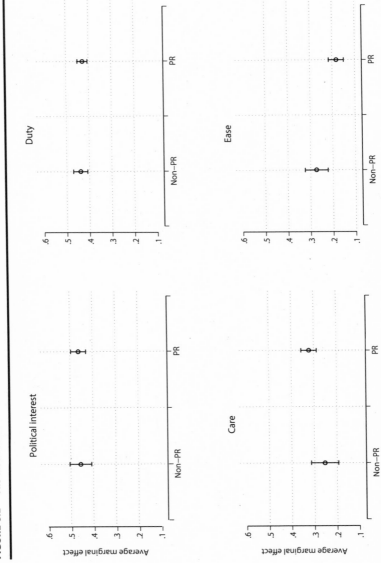

Notes: Effects are estimated from four separate logistic regressions. The 95% confidence intervals are included.

FIGURE 8.3 The motivation to vote in different levels of election

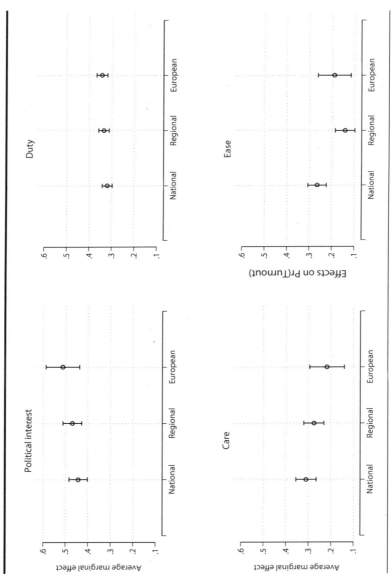

Notes: Effects are estimated from four separate logistic regressions. The 95% confidence intervals are included.

proportional representation (PR) from non-PR elections. The non-PR elections are those held in Canada and France except for the European election in France. With respect to the level, we distinguish European and regional elections from national ones.[3]

First, we run four separate logistic regressions examining the interaction of our four considerations with PR. We plot the average marginal effect of each consideration in PR and in non-PR elections in Figure 8.2. The effects of the two most powerful predispositions, political interest and duty, are almost identical in PR and non-PR elections. The impact of care is slightly higher and that of ease slightly lower in PR elections, but the differences in the marginal effects are modest. The big picture is clear: our model provides a powerful explanation of the turnout decision in both PR and non-PR elections.

Next, we run four separate logistic regressions examining the interaction of our four considerations with regional and European levels of election (the national level being the reference). Figure 8.3 shows the average marginal effect of each consideration across the three levels of election. Again there are some differences (ease seems to matter less in regional and European elections), but the differences are quite small. All in all, Figure 8.3 suggests that our model applies to all three levels.

The conventional wisdom in social research is that human behaviour is the outcome of a complex interplay of individual characteristics and contextual variables. We fully acknowledge that the decision to vote or abstain is not a purely individual one, that it is also affected by the characteristics of a given election. Our claim is rather that the most basic determinants are simply whether one likes politics or not and whether one does or does not construe voting as a moral obligation, and that the secondary factors are whether the person cares about the outcome and whether it is not too difficult to vote. These fundamental considerations are there all the time, and they come into play regardless of the specificities of the context.

Conclusion

Elections are an indispensable component of democracy. It is for very good reasons that the ordinary citizen's decision to participate or not in an election has been examined by a great number of political scientists. The literature has identified a myriad of factors that affect the decision to vote or abstain (for reviews, see Blais 2006; Geys 2006; Cancela and Geys 2016; Stockemer 2017).

Our goal has been to present a parsimonious, elegant, and compelling model of why people choose to vote or abstain in elections held in established democracies where voting is not compulsory. The argument is straightforward. It depends first and foremost on motivations. Most people vote most of the time because they want to and/or because they feel they ought to.

Many people, of course, do not like politics, and most of them are inclined to stay at home. But we should not lose sight of the fact that many people do like politics. The Making Electoral Democracy Work (MEDW) survey, like all surveys, reports a high general level of interest in politics. This level of interest is overstated since those who do not like politics are less likely to respond to political surveys, and there is a social desirability bias against indicating a low level of interest for almost anything. But political scientists may be prone to exaggerate the level of political disinterest, because of their expectation that everyone should share their passion, in the same way that those who are passionate about the arts or religion lament the public's lack of concern "for the most important or exciting thing in life." The bottom line is that quite a few people are genuinely (though not extremely) interested in politics and elections, and for these people voting is the normal thing to do.

The other major factor that motivates some people to vote is the belief that in a democracy voting is the right thing to do and abstaining is morally wrong – that is, a sense of civic duty. The feeling that one has the moral obligation to vote is profoundly paradoxical in a democracy, where the ideal of freedom of choice is paramount. Should not the democratic ideal entail the right to abstain?

The tension comes from the fact that the legitimacy of elections hinges in part on the degree of citizen participation; a high turnout is a public good. We thus hope that most people will decide to vote, even if they are not very interested, because society is better off with a "good" participation rate. This underlies the public norm that the good citizen should vote, that she has the duty to contribute at least minimally to the public good.

Those who feel that they have a duty to vote are likely to vote but the motivation is not quite as "natural" as for those who are very interested in politics. The dutiful person has to remind herself that her conscience tells her that she should vote, and she follows her conscience most of the time, especially if it is not too difficult.

As we indicated at the outset, we assume that lack of motivation is the main reason why some people do not vote. Ideally, we would need to understand where this lack of motivation comes from, but this requires a completely different study. The only point we wish to make is that we should not be surprised that some people are not very interested in politics and that some do not subscribe to the view that they have a moral duty to vote. There are so many things that require our attention and interest in life (politics, arts, sports, religion, family and friends, work, and so on) and we do not have the time and energy to maintain and nourish all these potential interests. Similarly, even though almost everyone agrees in principle with the idea that the good citizen should vote, there is also the dictum that we live in a free society and we therefore have the right not to participate, especially if we do not have clear preferences about the candidates or parties.

Our claim is that these two basic predispositions, one's level of interest in politics and one's feeling that voting is or is not a moral obligation, are the two most powerful individual-level determinants of the decision to vote or abstain. Because these predispositions are stable, there is strong stability in the propensity to vote. As a consequence, some people almost always vote while others almost always abstain. This stability is not the result of an acquired habit; it is simply the consequence of the fact that the act of voting reflects our priorities (how much we like politics relative to other "things") and values (our conception of our rights and duties in a democracy). Because our priorities and values seldom change, our predisposition to vote remains stable.

Predispositions are only predispositions. People who like politics tend to form strong preferences about the candidates and parties, which they will want to express on the ballot, while those who are uninterested tend not to care much about who will be elected. The match is far from perfect, however. As a consequence, whether one does or does not have clear preferences about the options in a specific election also matters, independent of one's initial predisposition. This is of course not surprising. What is perhaps less obvious is that it does not matter as much as general interest in politics and sense of civic duty.

Perhaps as obvious is the fact that people are less inclined to vote when voting is difficult or complicated. Less obvious is the finding that ease of voting does not matter that much. On the one hand, only one-fifth of the MEDW respondents indicate that it is somewhat or very difficult to vote (see Blais, Galais, and Coulombe 2019). This supports one of the main assumptions that underlie our analysis. The view that one has a duty to vote in an election makes sense only if there is a consensus about the central role that elections play in a democracy and if voting is easy, since it can then be argued that even if people have the "formal" right to abstain, they have a moral obligation to participate in a minimal way (voting) that takes little time and effort.

The literature on political participation usually emphasizes the role of resources (see, especially, Verba, Schlozman, and Brady 1995). We cannot tell whether this emphasis is justified in the case of non-electoral participation, but we are skeptical with respect to the decision to vote or abstain. The main reason is simply that voting is remarkably easy, as the overwhelming majority of MEDW respondents have told us, in response to the question about how easy or difficult it is to vote. Resources are necessary when there are obstacles to overcome. Except for a small minority or in exceptional circumstances, going to the polling station has become easier and easier. In fact, voting is one of the easiest human activities, much easier than working, playing sports, or going to a rock concert. If some people fail to vote some of the time, it is mainly because for them this is not a gratifying activity.

Voting may be easy, but what about gathering the information to help one decide which party to support? Is it not extremely difficult to become sufficiently informed? Not really. On the one hand, people can and do use all kinds of shortcuts to decide how to vote, and many of these shortcuts are widely available. On the other hand, people do find the time to become informed when they feel psychologically engaged. We know many people who have become experts in fashion, theatre, the Bible, organic food, football, the monarchy, design, the Middle Ages ... because they were passionate about the topic. Motivation is not everything, but it is a big part of the story.

That being said, we acknowledge the limitations of our analysis. We have relied on a single question that asked respondents to evaluate the overall ease/difficulty of voting. We do not know much about what underlies such judgments. The turnout literature has explored the impact of dozens of attitudes that affect the decision to vote or not to vote, but has neglected the role of potential and concrete hurdles that may provide incentives to stay at home. How many people find going to a polling station a physical challenge? How many people are sick and/or in some sort of psychological distress on election day? How many people are functional illiterates and do not quite understand what they are supposed to write on the ballot paper? We do not have reliable answers to these questions, which are extremely complicated to tackle since people who are ill or illiterate are unlikely to respond to surveys. We believe that there are relatively few people for whom voting is a challenge, but we must admit that we do not know much about them.

We have made the case in this study for an individual-level perspective on the determinants of turnout. We emphasize again that we do not dismiss the important role played by contextual-level variables. Our argument is simply that, all in all, individual-level factors matter more. In the MEDW data, only 5% of the variance in turnout can be accounted for by macro-level variables. As for interaction effects between contextual and individual factors, they certainly exist but their role may be overstated because it is fashionable to say that both sets of factors interact in complex ways. When we systematically test for them, we find only a few significant interactions.

There is, however, one aspect of individuals' context that we believe is absolutely crucial and that should be ideally incorporated in the analysis. This is their micro-context, most especially the household. In a fascinating study, David Cutts and Edward Fieldhouse (2009, 736) show that the propensity to vote increases dramatically if and when the other members of the household do vote, and that "those who live together in the same household have a strong tendency to vote together regardless of their political attitudes and interests, thus ruling out the argument that clustering is simply a product of the convergence of values and characteristics within households." Is the decision to vote or not an individual or household decision? To what extent do members of the household talk to each other about their intention to vote or not and the reasons for doing so? To what extent does the person who has a sense of civic duty put pressure on her partner who is inclined to stay home? These are fundamental questions for which we have no good data.

We indicated at the outset that our goal was to make sense of the decision to vote or not to vote in established democracies where voting is not compulsory. This raises the question of whether our model would need to be amended or completely revamped for the study of turnout in new or quasi democracies and/or when the law stipulates that voting is compulsory and there is some penalty associated with abstention. This would require a more systematic study, but we would like to share some initial thoughts.

Let us start with elections in quasi-democracies. We are thinking about situations where no elections had ever taken place, or where the previous elections were rigged in favour of the incumbent dictator. We suppose that the new election is more democratic than earlier ones, but the rules of the game are still biased in favour of the incumbent. In such a context, where things are moving rapidly, we would expect basic predispositions, such as interest and duty, not to matter as much, and the more specific considerations, such as care and ease of voting, to play a bigger role. In those situations, the issue of the election is not only about who will govern the country for the next four years or so but also about whether the country will move forward towards democratization. The stakes are higher, and this is clearly an additional incentive for going to the polls. At the same time, some people may suspect that the incumbent is certain to win the election, and this is obviously an incentive to abstain.[1]

What about compulsory voting? We assume that the compulsory voting law is not purely symbolic, that is, there are penalties for abstention without "good" reason, and that these penalties are at least minimally enforced. The obvious implication is that there is an additional consideration to be included in the analysis, which is the penalty that the person may have to incur if she abstains. This raises the question of whether citizens know what these penalties are and the likelihood that they will actually incur them if they decide not to vote. We are not aware of any systematic study of citizens' knowledge and perceptions of compulsory voting laws (but see Turgeon and Blais 2019). This also raises the question of whether the existence of a legal duty to vote strengthens or weakens sense of civic duty.[2] It also raises the thorny issue of whether sense of duty to vote should be measured differently when and where there is also a legal duty to vote. There are big challenges to studying the decision to vote or abstain in situations where the law stipulates that everyone is obliged to vote, but there are also great potential payoffs. We would learn a lot from a systematic comparison of what drives the turnout decision in the presence or absence of compulsory voting.

We hope to have convinced readers that the simple model proposed here, based on four considerations, two basic predispositions and two election-specific judgments, contributes to making sense of the decision to vote or abstain. The model is certainly not complete and cannot do full justice to the complexity of such a decision. Our claim is rather that this model makes sense, it is elegant, and it is supported by empirical evidence in a wide variety of contexts. It highlights the fact that the decision to vote reflects deep values about how much or how little we like politics and about the rights and duties of citizens in a democratic polity.

We hope that this study will trigger further research on a number of fronts. As mentioned above, our argument rests very much on the assumption that voting is, for the great majority of people, quite easy. We have provided empirical evidence to support our claim, but we need more extensive and intensive studies of the perceived cost of voting, with multiple indicators. Clearly our assumption does not hold for every individual and in every context, and we badly need precise accounts of what makes people view voting as easy or difficult.

We have placed much emphasis in our analysis on the central role of two basic predispositions, political interest and sense of civic duty. This raises the crucial question of the sources of these two predispositions. Fortunately, Markus Prior's monumental study (2019) provides precious insight about the factors that shape people's interest or disinterest in politics, but much further work is required to better understand what makes people come to the conclusion that politics is fun or not. We know much less about the sources of civic duty, and we need to fill that huge gap.

We end by stressing the importance of collecting good-quality survey data in order to understand citizens' motivations to vote or abstain. We have mainly used MEDW data, which included questions that were designed to measure as accurately as possible the considerations that do or do not drive people to the polls. This is particularly the case for sense of civic duty, which poses particular challenges.

We have used cross-sectional data to test our models. This is an important limitation of our study, as we would have much preferred to rely on panel data. This shortcoming is mitigated by the fact that there is relatively strong evidence that the two predispositions that are at the core of our interpretation, interest and duty, have been shown to be stable. The bottom line, however, is that we would be on stronger ground if we had longitudinal data.

The data that we have used are non-experimental, and quite a few readers might complain about that. We like experiments, we have used experiments in the past, and we will continue using experiments in future research. But experiments are not the only way to do research, and they are not the best approach for every research agenda. The bottom line is that if we want to make sense of people's decision to vote or not to vote, we need to understand their feelings, attitudes, and beliefs, and surveys provide precious information about these. The obvious solution is to combine field experiments with panel surveys. We invite researchers to explore such an avenue.

Some readers may wonder about the policy implications of our analysis. The most obvious implication is that if we want to increase voter turnout, we need to focus on citizens' motivations, directly in line with the title of this book, *The Motivation to Vote*. However, most efforts to increase citizens' participation in election are about reducing the costs of voting. Let us be clear: there is nothing wrong about efforts to make it easier to vote, and we strongly support such actions, while recognizing that their impact is likely to be limited (as we have seen, the vast majority of voters already perceive voting as being very easy).

We do need, however, to devote *at least* as much effort to make it more pleasant or exciting to vote. One way to foster such excitement is to make election day a special occasion when people can express their attachment to the country and to democracy. This objective can be achieved in many different concrete ways. From this perspective, it makes sense to make election day a holiday to be celebrated. It also makes sense to hold elections around the same time of the year and not too often (the less frequent an event is, the more special it is). This is an argument in favour of fixed election dates.

Voting must be perceived to be fun, and fun is something we share with relatives and friends. Everything should be done to encourage people to invite their friends and relatives to go and vote together. We should make it as easy and attractive as possible for family members to go together to the polling station. Why not have special voting booths for the kids to familiarize them with the democratic system and serve coffee, juice, and cookies to make it even more pleasant? Since many polling stations are located in schools, local school boards could have a "café" (with daycare), where people can have coffee or tea after fulfilling their civic duty, while chatting with others in their neighbourhood. Or why not allow "selfies" so people can show their friends that they voted and are happy to share the experience?

An election is a precious moment when we are reminded that we belong to a collectivity, that there are issues that need to be addressed through collective action, and that it makes sense to have an election to choose those who will make these collective decisions. There are good reasons to want to participate, and we should nourish the motivation to do so.

Appendices

APPENDIX 1: WORDING OF QUESTIONS

Age

In what year were you born?

Education

What is the highest level of education that you have completed?

- ☐ No schooling
- ☐ Some elementary school
- ☐ Completed elementary school
- ☐ Some secondary/high school
- ☐ Completed secondary/high school
- ☐ Some technical, community
- ☐ Completed technical, community
- ☐ Some university
- ☐ Bachelor's degree
- ☐ Master's degree
- ☐ Professional degree or doctorate
- ☐ Don't know

Political Interest

On a scale from 0 to 10, where 0 means "no interest at all" and 10 means "a great deal of interest," how much interest do you have in the current federal election?

Duty

If you didn't vote in this election, would you personally feel very guilty, somewhat guilty, not very guilty, or not guilty at all?

☐ Very guilty
☐ Somewhat guilty
☐ Not very guilty
☐ Not guilty at all
☐ Don't know

Care

On a scale from 0 to 10, where 0 means that you "don't care at all" and 10 means that you "care a lot," how much do you care which party will form the government in [NAME OF THE COUNTRY OR REGION] after the election?

Ease

For some people voting is a simple and easy thing to do. For others, it is difficult or inconvenient. For you personally, how easy or difficult is it to vote?

☐ Very difficult
☐ Somewhat difficult
☐ Somewhat easy
☐ Very easy
☐ Don't know

Turnout

Treatment A. Did you vote on election day or at an advance poll or by special measures?

☐ Yes
☐ No
☐ Don't know/prefer not to answer

Treatment B. In each election we find that a lot of people were not able to vote because they were not registered, they were sick, or they did not have time. Which of the following statements best describes you?

☐ I did not vote in the election
☐ I thought about voting this time but didn't
☐ I usually vote but didn't this time
☐ I am sure I voted in the election
☐ Don't know/prefer not to answer

APPENDIX 2: ADDITIONAL TABLES

TABLE A.1   The elections and the turnout rate

Elections	*N* before weight	*N* after weight	Turnout (%)
Switzerland			
Lucerne national 2011	823	836	53
Lucerne regional 2011	873	863	50
Zurich national 2011	820	836	44
Zurich regional 2011	809	800	35
France			
Paris national 2012	716	713	54
Paris municipal 2014	824	819	55
Provence national 2012	701	701	56
Provence Europe 2014	775	777	43
Paris Europe 2014	774	782	43
Marseille municipal 2014	497	496	50
Spain			
Catalonia national 2011	790	791	66
Catalonia regional 2012	773	763	70
Madrid national 2011	799	800	73
Madrid regional 2015	744	736	66
Germany			
Lower Saxony national 2013	723	746	73
Lower Saxony regional 2013	765	756	59
Lower Saxony Europe 2014	737	739	49
Bavaria national 2013	3,575	3,628	70
Bavaria regional 2013	4,261	4,214	64
Canada			
Ontario national 2015	1,334	1,328	68
Ontario regional 2011	861	851	49
Quebec national 2015	1,223	1,232	66
Quebec regional 2012	693	685	75
British Columbia national 2015	1,215	1,212	70
Total	26,105	≈26,105	61

TABLE A.2   The determinants of turnout: impact of question wording

	(Model 1)	(Model 2)	(Model 3)	(Model 4)
Age	1.25***	1.24***	1.25***	1.25***
	(0.19)	(0.19)	(0.19)	(0.19)
Post-secondary education	0.34***	0.34***	0.34***	0.34***
	(0.07)	(0.07)	(0.07)	(0.07)
Political interest	0.63**	0.55**	0.55**	0.54**
	(0.24)	(0.20)	(0.20)	(0.20)
Duty	1.95***	1.80***	1.95***	1.95***
	(0.08)	(0.12)	(0.08)	(0.08)
Care	1.17***	1.17***	0.93***	1.17***
	(0.15)	(0.15)	(0.23)	(0.15)
Ease of voting	1.31***	1.30***	1.31***	1.31***
	(0.14)	(0.14)	(0.14)	(0.13)
Treatment	−0.49***	−0.70***	−0.90***	−0.57***
	(0.11)	(0.09)	(0.16)	(0.12)
Treatment × political interest	−0.16			
	(0.16)			
Treatment × duty		0.28		
		(0.19)		
Treatment × care			0.47*	
			(0.22)	
Treatment × ease of voting				−0.01
				(0.13)
Constant	−2.95***	−2.83***	−2.74***	−2.90***
	(0.17)	(0.14)	(0.17)	(0.14)
Observations	17,546	17,546	17,546	17,546
Pseudo R^2	.244	.244	.245	.244

Notes: Entries are logistic regression coefficients. Robust standard errors, clustered by election, are in parentheses. Election fixed effects are included.
* $p < .05$, ** $p < .01$, *** $p < .001$

TABLE A.3   The determinants of turnout: unweighted data

	(Model 1)	(Model 2)	(Model 3)	(Model 4)	(Model 5)	(Model 6)
Age	1.82*** (0.14)	1.96*** (0.15)	1.55*** (0.16)	1.52*** (0.15)	1.44*** (0.14)	1.25*** (0.15)
Post-secondary education		0.56*** (0.06)	0.40*** (0.05)	0.33*** (0.06)	0.34*** (0.06)	0.32*** (0.06)
Political interest			2.33*** (0.14)	1.36*** (0.16)	0.79*** (0.17)	0.65*** (0.16)
Duty				2.17*** (0.07)	1.88*** (0.06)	1.85*** (0.06)
Care					1.47*** (0.14)	1.38*** (0.14)
Ease of voting						1.13*** (0.14)
Constant	0.85*** (0.05)	0.69*** (0.06)	−0.64*** (0.08)	−0.97*** (0.08)	−1.41*** (0.09)	−1.99*** (0.12)
Observations	26,105	26,105	26,105	26,105	26,105	26,105
Pseudo R^2	.069	.078	.127	.190	.203	.214

Notes: Entries are logistic regression coefficients. Robust standard errors, clustered by election, are in parentheses. Election fixed effects are included.
* $p < .05$, ** $p < .01$, *** $p < .001$

TABLE A.4   The determinants of turnout: interaction effects

	(Model 1)	(Model 2)	(Model 3)
Age	1.34***	1.37***	1.34***
	(0.15)	(0.15)	(0.15)
Post-secondary education	0.33***	0.33***	0.33***
	(0.06)	(0.06)	(0.06)
Political interest	0.64***	0.61***	0.60***
	(0.18)	(0.16)	(0.16)
Duty	1.99***	2.72***	1.91***
	(0.21)	(0.16)	(0.06)
Care	1.40***	1.73***	1.09***
	(0.18)	(0.20)	(0.27)
Ease of voting	1.14***	1.16***	0.84***
	(0.18)	(0.18)	(0.21)
Political interest × duty	−0.11		
	(0.32)		
Duty × care		−1.09***	
		(0.22)	
Care × ease of voting			0.45
			(0.28)
Constant	−3.32***	−3.54***	−3.09***
	(0.15)	(0.19)	(0.20)
Observations	26,105	26,105	26,105
Pseudo R^2	.229	.230	.229

Notes: Entries are logistic regression coefficients. Robust standard errors, clustered by election, are in parentheses. Election fixed effects are included.
* $p < .05$, ** $p < .01$, *** $p < .001$

TABLE A.5   **The impact of habit: replication of the 1980 ANES using validated vote**

	(Model 1)	(Model 2)
Consistency =	Always	Always or never
Age	0.84**	1.09***
	(0.27)	(0.26)
Woman	−0.13	−0.10
	(0.12)	(0.12)
Education	0.29*	0.47***
	(0.13)	(0.13)
Political interest	0.99***	0.80***
	(0.21)	(0.23)
PID (party identification)	1.36***	0.89***
	(0.24)	(0.27)
Care	−0.07	0.10
	(0.16)	(0.17)
Civic duty	0.14	0.42*
	(0.15)	(0.17)
Consistency	2.06***	−0.01
	(0.35)	(0.29)
Consistency × political interest	−0.24	0.58
	(0.36)	(0.34)
Consistency × PID	−1.66***	−0.04
	(0.43)	(0.37)
Consistency × care	0.32	−0.15
	(0.27)	(0.25)
Consistency × duty	0.11	−0.22
	(0.26)	(0.24)
Constant	−1.86***	−1.52***
	(0.20)	(0.23)
Observations	1,406	1,406
Pseudo R^2	.147	.105

Notes: Entries are logistic regression coefficients. Robust standard errors are in parentheses.
* $p < .05$, ** $p < .01$, *** $p < .001$

Notes

Chapter 1: The Decision to Vote or Not to Vote

1   In a presidential election, people vote for a candidate (usually associated with a party). In a legislative election, they vote for a candidate (usually associated with a party), for a party, or both. Though there is growing evidence about the personalization of the vote (Clarke et al. 2004; Bittner 2011; Marsh 2007), the fact is that most people vote, implicitly or explicitly, for a party. For the sake of simplicity, we characterize an election as entailing a choice among parties, though it is also a choice among candidates.

2   We assume that voting takes place in the polling station, which is the case for an overwhelming majority of citizens. In one of the countries included in this study (Switzerland), most people vote by mail, which of course makes voting much easier, but the ballot paper is much more complicated. See Chapter 6 for a more elaborate discussion.

3   We added the province of British Columbia in the case of the 2015 Canadian election.

4   We could not include the European election in Catalonia, Madrid, and Bavaria because our measure of duty was not asked in those surveys.

5   The overall turnout in the first round of the 2014 French municipal elections was 59%, compared with 50% for the 2015 regional elections. Turnout in the second round of the 2015 regional elections surged to 58% as the big success of the Front National in the first round motivated many to show up at the polls to block the party.

6   In some sense, the 2014 European election could also be counted as one, but it is more appropriate to construe it as a separate election in each country, since the party systems were completely different.

7   For a description, see Dolez, Laurent, and Blais (2017).

8   The experiment was not performed in three of the twenty-four elections – Lower Saxony national, and Bavaria national and regional.

9   In other words, we assume that the biases in our sample of abstainers are similar to the biases in our sample of voters.

10 The patterns are the same with respect to the logistic coefficients. The estimated marginal effects (in terms of predicted probabilities) are systematically lower with the unweighted data because of the presence of ceiling effects. The logistic coefficients are unaffected by these ceiling effects (see Blais and Achen 2019).

11 We use the regional election in Lower Saxony because turnout in that election was close to the mean turnout in the twenty-four elections. It is thus a "typical" election with respect to the dependent variable.

12 This is of course because we are interested in explaining why some people vote while others abstain. Individual-level variables are much less relevant when it comes to explaining why overall turnout is higher in some elections than in others.

13 We would need to have treatments for which there is a clear expectation that they shape specific motivations, and we would need to test that expectation with survey data. For an example, see Holbein (2017).

14 See Galais and Blais (2016) for an interesting exception.

Chapter 2: Who Votes?

1   The authors do not estimate or compare the magnitude of the effects associated with each variable.

2   Hobbs and colleagues (2014) show that widowed individuals vote 9 percentage points less than they would have had their spouse still been living, and that variations in the "widowhood effect" support a social isolation explanation for the turnout drop.

3   We have tested models adding age^2 (and age^2 and age^3), and the coefficients associated with these additional terms were not significant.

4   For the relationship between health and turnout, see Mattila et al. (2013), Ojeda and Pacheco (2019), and Sund et al. (2017). We have less confidence in the representativeness of the sample among those aged over 75, who tend to be more educated than in reality.

5   Only 36% of those aged 18–24 have a post-secondary education, but this is so because many are still in the process of completing their studies.

6   As in all the analyses where turnout is the dependent variable, we include election fixed effects.

7 More precisely, the mean predicted probability of voting in our sample would be .64 if everyone had a post-secondary education while keeping the same value on the other independent variables (in this case, age), and .53 if everyone had no post-secondary education while keeping the same value on the other independent variables. We use the same approach throughout the study to ascertain the independent marginal effect of specific variables.

8 As in all observational studies, we cannot rule out the possibility that some of the relationships that we report are biased or even spurious. Our approach is to minimize the risk by controlling for the most powerful antecedent variables. At the same time, we are strong believers in parsimonious models, and we are thus including as few controls as possible.

Chapter 3: Do I Like Politics?

1 See Appendix 1 for the exact wording of the question.

2 These biases are attenuated by the fact that the data are weighted so that abstainers (who are generally less interested) have a greater weight. Still, the overall level of interest reported in the MEDW election surveys is slightly higher than that reported in the non-political household surveys, which are the main source of data used by Prior (2018).

3 We compare individuals aged 30 and 60 to illustrate the impact of age. As the mean age in the sample is 46 and the standard deviation is 14, we are thus comparing individuals who are 1 standard deviation above and below the mean.

4 We compare individuals who are 1 standard deviation under and above the mean. The mean is .6 and the standard deviation .3.

Chapter 4: Do I Have a Duty to Vote?

1 Note that the parties or politicians that may benefit from a lower turnout would have an opposite interest.

2 This is so in a large community where direct democracy is not possible. One could argue that a lottery in which all citizens have an equal probability of being chosen is equally democratic. But since the lottery is not used for the selection of legislators in contemporary democracies, elections remain a necessary condition.

3 People were asked whether they agree or disagree with the statement on a 0-to-10 scale, where 0 means fully disagree and 10 means fully agree. The mean (and median) score was 7. The question was included in an Internet

survey conducted in seven European countries (with a total sample size of 20,000) after the 2014 European election. The survey was an initiative of the Centre d'études européennes de Sciences Po (principal investigator: Nicolas Sauger). See Blais and Galais (2016, Appendix 1).

4 For instance, in the 1960 US presidential election, the difference in the turnout rate between the low- and high-duty respondents among those who are low on the other two variables (P and B) is 25 percentage points. The equivalent differences between the low and high on B and P are 19 and 4 points, respectively.

5 The same verdict applies to party identification. Ideally, we would like to manipulate it to see how it affects vote choice, but that is practically impossible.

6 We treat duty as unconditional, that is, people feel that they have a moral obligation to vote in every election, whatever the context. Nicole Goodman (2018) has argued that sense of duty may be conditional, that is, people believe that they have a duty to vote only in some circumstances. Clearly duty cannot be purely unconditional (most people think that there is no duty to vote when one is very sick) or purely conditional (there are many people who feel they should vote in *every* election). We note the following: (1) Goodman's questions are all agree/disagree items, which is problematic; (2) in her study, only a minority of respondents agreed with her "conditional duty" items, while a majority agreed with the "traditional" items; (3) duty has been shown to be quite stable over time and to differ little across types of elections (Galais and Blais 2016), which should not be the case if people feel that they have a duty to vote only under some circumstances. That being said, we recognize that for some people duty may be conditional and that more work is required to investigate such conditionality.

7 No single question can perfectly measure sense of duty (or any attitude for that matter), and so there are some dutiful people who would not feel guilty (or who would not acknowledge that they feel guilty!), but we are confident that there are few of them.

8 In the English version, having a duty is implicitly portrayed as having no choice. This makes sense since when our conscience tells us that we have a moral obligation to vote, we feel that we have no choice but to follow our conscience.

9 Note that the effects of age and education are only slightly reduced when duty is introduced in the model.

Chapter 5: Do I Care about the Outcome?

1 The question was slightly different in the case of European elections, which do not lead to the formation of a government, and then simply referred to the outcome of the election.

2 The objective power of the European Union relative to that of national governments is debatable. What is clear, however, is that most people perceive the European Union to have less direct impact on their lives than their national government. The MEDW questionnaire included the following question: "On a scale from 0 to 10, where 0 means a very small impact and 10 means a very big impact, how much influence do the policies of the following governments have on the well-being of you and your family?" In each of the three EU countries covered by our study, the mean impact score given to the national government is about 6, while that of the EU is about 5. See Golder et al. (2017, 71–72).

3 Note, however, that the regional elections that we cover may be deemed particularly meaningful because of the presence of strong decentralization and/or nationalist movements.

4 Scores of .5 and 1 correspond to values 1 standard deviation (.25) under and above the mean score of .74.

5 The 15-percentage-point effect is much smaller than that of duty and interest.

6 The question was not asked in Spain and in the German national election.

Chapter 6: Is It Easy to Vote?

1 There have been a few studies in the United States about waiting time (see Stewart III 2012; Pettigrew 2017; and Stein et al. 2019).

2 See Blais, Galais, and Coulombe (2019) for a presentation and discussion of the results.

3 It reduced voting at the polling stations by 3 points, but this was partially compensated by a 1-point increase in absentee voting.

4 For an attempt to distinguish these two types of cost, see Blais, Galais, and Coulombe (2019). The authors find that the direct costs (those related to the act of voting) matter more than the information/decision costs.

5 There is no evidence of a non-linear effect.

Chapter 7: Is Voting a Habit?

1 This is the very first definition proposed by Dictionary.com. See http://www.dictionary.com/browse/habit.

2 It is worth noting that habit had been mentioned as a possibility in *The American Voter* (Campbell et al. 1960, 92): "It is possible to think of voting as a type of conduct that is somewhat habitual."

3 The reasoning is that it takes about three elections to form a habit. As there is a national election every three years on average, this means about ten years. As mentioned in Chapter 1, most citizens have to decide whether to vote or not about once per year, if we take into account subnational and supranational elections as well as referenda.

4 In 1998, canvassing boosted participation by 10 percentage points while the mail effect was 1.5 percentage points.

5 This is explicitly acknowledged by Fieldhouse and Cutts (2012, 858).

6 Dinas (2012) does consider information and party identification, however.

7 The authors' dependent variable is a dummy that equals 1 for those who voted in each of the four elections or who abstained in all four elections. Note that they interpret voting or abstaining in each of two rounds of presidential and legislative elections that took place in a period of two months as an indication of habit. This is as if we were to conclude, after having seen a friend go to the gym once a week for four consecutive weeks, that she had acquired the habit of exercising.

8 CSES datasets do not include measures of interest, duty, care, and cost.

9 Aldrich, Montgomery, and Wood (2011) assume that there are no habitual abstainers.

10 As mentioned above, experimental studies could demonstrate the presence of inertia if they were combined with survey data that include measures of attitudes such as interest and duty, and indicated that previous voting has an independent effect on turnout, independent of these attitudes. We are not aware of any such study combining a field experiment and survey data.

Chapter 8: Does It All Depend on the Context?

1 We are contrasting individuals' characteristics with those of the elections, in the same way as in Mark Franklin (2004). Context may mean many different things. We have in mind the context of the election, the electoral system, the party system, the degree of competitiveness, or the salience of the issues. We have no doubt that individuals' immediate environment (most especially the family) has an important effect, especially in shaping predispositions such as level of political interest and sense of civic duty.

2 This is within established democracies. We would expect sense of civic duty to be weaker in less democratic countries (see Galais and Blais 2017).

3 The Marseille municipal election is included among regional elections.

Conclusion

1 Ora John Reuter (2019) has an intriguing analysis of the role of civic duty in Russia, where the duty to vote is linked to patriotism.

2 Arturo Maldonado (2015) explores this issue.

References

Achen, Christopher, and André Blais. 2016. "Intention to Vote, Reported Vote, and Validated Vote." In *The Act of Voting: Identities, Institutions, and Locale,* ed. Johan A. Elkink and David M. Farrell, 195–209. London: Routledge.

Aldrich, John H., Jacob M. Montgomery, and Wendy Wood. 2011. "Turnout as a Habit." *Political Behaviour* 33: 535–63.

Anderson, Christopher J., and Russell J. Dalton. 2011. "Nested Voters: Citizen Choices Embedded in Political Contexts." In *Citizens, Context, and Choice: How Context Shapes Citizens' Electoral Choices,* ed. Russell J. Dalton and Christopher J. Anderson, 257–68. Oxford: Oxford University Press.

Bechtel, Michael, Dominik Hangartner, and Lukas Schmid. 2018. "Compulsory Voting, Habit Formation, and Political Participation." *Review of Economics and Statistics* 100 (3): 467–76.

Bergh, Johannes. 2013. "Does Voting Rights Affect the Political Maturity of 16 and 17-Year-Olds? Findings from the 2011 Norwegian Voting-Age Trial." *Electoral Studies* 32 (1): 90–100.

Bhatti, Yosef, and Kasper M. Hansen. 2012. "Leaving the Nest and the Social Act of Voting: Turnout among First-Time Voters." *Journal of Elections, Public Opinion and Parties* 22: 380–406.

Bhatti, Yosef, Kasper M. Hansen, and Hanna Wass. 2012. "The Relationship between Age and Turnout: A Roller-Coaster Ride." *Electoral Studies* 31 (3): 588–93.

Birch, Sarah. 2009. *Full Participation: A Comparative Study of Compulsory Voting.* Manchester: Manchester University Press.

Bittner, Amanda. 2011. *Platform or Personality? The Role of Party Leaders in Elections.* Oxford: Oxford University Press.

Blais, André. 2000. *To Vote or Not to Vote? The Merits and Limits of Rational Choice Theory.* Pittsburgh: University of Pittsburgh Press.

–. 2006. "What Affects Turnout?" *Annual Review of Political Science* 9: 111–25.

–. 2010a. "Making Electoral Democracy Work." *Electoral Studies* 29: 169–70.

–. 2010b. "Political Participation." In *Comparing Democracies: Elections and Voting in the 21st Century,* ed. Lawrence LeDuc, Richard G. Niemi, and Pippa Norris, 165–83. Los Angeles: Sage.

–. 2014. "Why Is Turnout So Low in Switzerland? Comparing the Attitudes of Swiss and German Citizens Towards Electoral Democracy." *Swiss Political Science Review* 20 (4): 520–28.

–. 2015. "Rational Choice and the Calculus of Voting." In *Handbook of Social Choice and Voting,* ed. Jac C. Heckelman and Nicholas R. Miller, 54–66. Cheltenham, UK: Edward Elgar.

–. 2018. *Voter Turnout: A Researcher's Perspective.* Cascais: Portugal Talks.

Blais, André, and Kees Aarts. 2006. "Electoral Systems and Turnout." *Acta Politica* 41: 180–96.

Blais, André, and Chris Achen. 2019. "Civic Duty and Voter Turnout." *Political Behavior* 41 (2): 473–97.

Blais, André, and Jean-François Daoust. 2017. "What Do Voters Do When They Like a Local Candidate from Another Party?" *Canadian Journal of Political Science* 50 (4): 1103–9.

Blais, André, Jean-François Daoust, Ruth Dassonneville, and Gabrielle Péloquin-Skulski. 2019. "What Is the Cost of Voting?" *Electoral Studies* 59: 145–57.

Blais, André, and Agnieszka Dobrzynska. 1998. "Turnout in Electoral Democracies." *European Journal of Political Research* 33: 239–61.

Blais, André, and Carol Galais. 2016. "Measuring the Civic Duty to Vote: A Proposal." *Electoral Studies* 41: 60–69.

Blais, André, Carol Galais, and Maxime Coulombe. 2019. "The Effect of Social Pressure from Family and Friends on Turnout." *Journal of Social and Personal Relationships* 36 (9): 2824–41.

Blais, André, Carol Galais, and Danielle Mayer. 2019. "Is There a Duty to Vote *and* Be Informed?" *Political Studies Review.* Available at https://doi.org/10.1177%2F1478929919865467.

Blais, André, Elisabeth Gidengil, Richard Nadeau, and Neil Nevitte. 2002. *Anatomy of a Liberal Victory: Making Sense of the Vote in the 2000 Canadian Election.* Peterborough, ON: Broadview Press.

Blais, André, Elisabeth Gidengil, Neil Nevitte, and Richard Nadeau. 2004. "Where Does Turnout Decline Come From?" *European Journal of Political Research* 43: 221–36.

Blais, André, and Daniel Rubenson. 2013. "The Source of Turnout Decline: New Values or New Contexts?" *Comparative Political Studies* 46 (1): 95–117.

Brady, Henry, and John McNulty. 2011. "Turning Out to Vote: The Costs of Finding and Getting to the Polling Place." *American Political Science Review* 105: 115–34.

Brady, Henry, Sidney Verba, and Kay L. Schlozman. 1995. "Beyond SES: A Resource Model of Political Participation." *American Political Science Review* 89 (2): 271–94.

Brambor, Thomas, William Clark, and Matt Golder. 2006. "Understanding Interaction Models: Improving Empirical Analyses." *Political Analysis* 14: 63–82.

Brennan, G., and J.M. Buchanan. 1984. "Voter Choice: Evaluating Political Alternatives." *American Behavioral Scientist* 28: 185–201.

Brennan G., and A. Hamlin. 1998. "Expressive Voting and Electoral Equilibrium." *Public Choice* 95: 149–75.

Brennan G., and L. Lomasky. 1997. *Democracy and Decision: The Pure Theory of Electoral Preference.* Cambridge: Cambridge University Press.

Campbell, Angus, Philip E. Converse, Warren E. Miller, and Donald E. Stokes. 1960. *The American Voter.* Chicago: University of Chicago Press.

Campbell, Angus, Gerald Gurin, and Warren E. Miller. 1954. *The Voter Decides.* Evanston, IL: Row, Peterson.

Campbell, David E. 2006. *Why We Vote: How Schools and Communities Shape Our Civic Life.* Princeton, NJ: Princeton University Press.

Cancela, João, and Benny Geys. 2016. "Explaining Voter Turnout: A Meta-Analysis of National and Subnational Elections." *Electoral Studies* 42: 264–75.

Clarke, Harold D., David Sanders, Marianne C. Stewart, and Paul Whiteley. 2004. *Political Choice in Britain.* Oxford: Oxford University Press.

Coppock, Alexander, and Donald P. Green. 2017. "Is Voting Habit Forming? New Evidence from Experiments and Regression Discontinuities." *American Journal of Political Science* 60 (4): 1044–62.

Cox, James. 2004. "How to Identify Trust and Reciprocity." *Games and Economic Behavior* 46 (2): 260–81.

Cutts, David, and Edward Fieldhouse. 2009. "What Small Spatial Scales Are Relevant as Electoral Contexts for Individual Voters? The Importance of the Household on Turnout at the 2001 General Election." *American Journal of Political Science* 53: 726–39.

Cutts, David, Edward Fieldhouse, and Peter John. 2009. "Is Voting Habit Forming? The Longitudinal Impact of a GOTV Campaign in the UK." *Journal of Elections, Public Opinion and Parties* 19 (3): 251–63.

Dalton, Russell J. 2008. *The Good Citizen*. Washington, DC: Congressional Quarterly Press.

Dalton, Russell J., and Christopher J. Anderson, eds. 2011. *Citizens, Context, and Choice: How Context Shapes Electoral Choices*. Oxford: Oxford University Press.

Daoust, Jean-François, and André Blais. 2017. "How Much Do Voters Care about the Electoral Outcomes in Their District?" *Representation* 53 (3–4): 233–46.

Dennis, J. 1970. "Support for the Institutions of Elections by the Public." *American Political Science Review* 64: 919–35.

Denny, Kevin, and Orla Doyle. 2009. "Does Voting History Matter? Analysing Persistence in Turnout." *American Journal of Political Science* 53 (1): 17–35.

Dinas, Elias. 2012. "The Formation of Voting Habits." *Journal of Elections, Public Opinion and Parties* 22 (4): 431–56.

Dolez, Bernard, Annie Laurent, and André Blais. 2017. "Strategic Voting in the Second Round of a Two-Round System: The 2014 French Municipal Election." *French Politics* 15 (1): 27–42.

Dormagen, Jean-Yves, and Laura Michel. 2017. "Aging, Habit and Turnout: New Evidence from 12 Voting Rounds in France." Paper presented at the Annual Meeting of the American Political Science Association, San Francisco.

Downs, Anthony. 1957. *An Economic Theory of Democracy*. New York: Harper.

Druckman, James N., and Thomas J. Leeper. 2012. "Learning from Political Communication Experiments: Pretreatment and Its Effects." *American Journal of Political Science* 56 (4): 875–96.

Dufwenberg, Martin, and Georg Kirchsteiger. 2004. "A Theory of Sequential Reciprocity." *Games and Economic Behavior* 47 (2): 268–98.

Dyck, J.J., and J.G. Gimpel. 2005. "Distance, Turnout, and the Convenience of Voting." *Social Science Quarterly* 86: 531–48.

Elections Canada. 2012. "Estimation of Voter Turnout by Age Group and Gender at the 2011 Federal General Election." Available at http://www.elections.ca/content.aspx?section=res&dir=rec/part/estim/41ge&document=report41&lang=e.

Falk, Armin, and Urs Fischbacher. 2006. "A Theory of Reciprocity." *Games and Economic Behavior* 54 (2): 293–315.

Feitosa, Fernando, and Carol Galais. 2019. "How Stable Is Sense of Civic Duty? A Panel Study on the Individual-Level Stability of the Attitude." *International Journal of Public Opinion Research*. Available at https://doi.org/10.1093/ijpor/edz029.

Fieldhouse, Edward, and David Cutts. 2012. "The Companion Effect: Household and Local Context and Turnout of Young People." *Journal of Politics* 74 (3): 856–69.

Franklin, Mark N. 2004. *Voter Turnout and the Dynamics of Electoral Competition in Established Democracies since 1945.* Cambridge: Cambridge University Press.

Fujiwara, Thomas, Kyle Meng, and Tom Vogl. 2016. "Habit Formation in Voting: Evidence from Rainy Elections." *American Economic Journal: Applied Economics* 8 (4): 160–88.

Galais, Carol, and André Blais. 2014. "A Call of Duty in Hard Times: Duty to Vote and the Spanish Economic Crisis." *Research and Politics* 1: 1–8.

–. 2016a. "Beyond Rationalization: Voting Out of Duty or Expressing Duty after Voting?" *International Political Science Review* 37: 213–29.

–. 2016b. "Do People Feel More of a Duty to Vote in Some Elections?" *West European Politics* 39: 755–77.

–. 2017. "Duty to Vote and Political Support in Asia." *International Journal of Public Opinion Research* 29: 631–56.

Gallego, Aina. 2015. *Unequal Political Participation Worldwide.* New York: Cambridge University Press.

Gerber, Alan S., Donald P. Green, and Christopher W. Larimer. 2008. "Social Pressure and Voter Turnout: Evidence from a Large-Scale Field Experiment." *American Political Science Review* 102 (1): 33–48.

Gerber, Alan S., Donald P. Green, and Ron Shachar. 2003. "Voting May Be Habit-Forming: Evidence from a Randomized Field Experiment." *American Journal of Political Science* 47 (3): 540–50.

Geys, Benny. 2006. "Explaining Voter Turnout: A Review of Aggregate-Level Research." *Electoral Studies* 25: 637–63.

Gimpel, J.G., J.J. Dyck, and R.S. Daron. 2006. "Location, Knowledge and Time Pressures in the Spatial Structure of Convenience Voting." *Electoral Studies* 25 (1): 35–58.

Gimpel, J.G., J.C. Lay, and J.E. Schuknecht. 2003. *Cultivating Democracy: Civic Environments and Political Socialization in America*. Washington, DC: Brookings Institution Press.

Golder, Sona N., Ignacio Lago, André Blais, Elisabeth Gidengil, and Thomas Gschwend. 2017. *Multi-Level Electoral Politics: Beyond the Second-Order Election Model*. Oxford: Oxford University Press.

Goodman, Nicole. 2018. "The Conditional Duty to Vote in Elections." *Electoral Studies* 53: 39–47.

Groves, Robert, Stanley Presser, and Sarah Dipko. 2004. "The Role of Topic Interest in Survey Participation Decisions." *Public Opinion Quarterly* 68: 2–31.

Hibbing, John R., and Elizabeth Theiss-Morse. 2002. *Stealth Democracy: Americans' Beliefs about How Government Should Work*. Cambridge: Cambridge University Press.

Hobbs, William R., Nicholas A. Christakis, and James H. Fowler. 2014. "Widowhood Effects in Voter Participation." *American Journal of Political Science* 58: 1–16.

Holbein, John B. 2017. "Childhood Skill Development and Adult Political Participation." *American Political Science Review* 111 (3): 572–83.

Holbein, John B., and Sunshine Hillygus. 2016. "Making Young Voters: The Impact of Preregistration on Youth Turnout." *American Journal of Political Science* 60 (2): 364–82.

Jennings, M. Kent, Gregory B. Markus, and Richard G. Niemi. 1991. *Youth-Parent Socialization Panel Study, 1965–1982: Three Waves Combined*. Ann Arbor: University of Michigan, Center for Political Studies/Survey Research Center.

Jennings, M. Kent, Gregory B. Markus, Richard G. Niemi, and Laura Stoker. 2005. *Youth-Parent Socialization Panel Study, 1965–1997: Four Waves Combined*. Ann Arbor: University of Michigan, Center for Political Studies/Survey Research Center.

Kittilson, Miki Caul, and Christopher J. Anderson. 2011. "Electoral Supply and Voter Turnout." In *Citizens, Context, and Choice: How Context Shapes*

Electoral Choices, ed. Russell J. Dalton and Christopher J. Anderson, 33–44. Oxford: Oxford University Press.

Kostelka, Filip. 2015. "To Mobilise and Demobilise: The Puzzling Decline of Voter Turnout in Post-Communist Democracies." PhD dissertation, Institute of Political Studies, Paris.

Krosnick, Jon A. 1999. "Survey Research." *Annual Review of Psychology* 50: 537–67.

Kugler, K.E., and W.H. Jones. 1992. "On Conceptualization and Assessing Guilt." *Journal of Personality and Social Psychology* 62: 318–27.

Leighley, Jan E., and Jonathan Nagler. 2014. *Who Votes Now? Demographics, Issues, Inequality, and Turnout in the United States.* Princeton, NJ: Princeton University Press.

Lewis-Beck, M.S., W.G. Jacoby, H. Norpoth, and H.F. Weisberg. 2008. *The American Voter Revisited.* Ann Arbor: University of Michigan Press.

Maldonado. Arturo. 2015. "The Origins and Consequences of Compulsory Voting in Latin America." PhD dissertation, Vanderbilt University.

Marsh, Michael. 2007. "Candidates of Parties? Objects of Electoral Choice in Ireland." *Party Politics* 13: 500–27.

Massicotte Louis, André Blais, and Antoine Yoshinaka. 2004. *Establishing the Rules of the Game: Election Laws in Democracies.* Toronto: University of Toronto Press.

Mattila, Miko, Peter Söderlund, Hanna Wass, and Lauri Rapelli. 2013. "Healthy Voting: The Effect of Self-Reported Health on Turnout in 30 Countries." *Electoral Studies* 32 (4): 886–91.

Meredith, Marc. 2009. "Persistence in Political Participation." *Quarterly Journal of Political Science* 4 (3): 187–209.

Milbrath, Lester W., and Madan L. Goel. 1977. *Political Participation.* Chicago: Rand McNally.

Miller, Warren E., and J. Merrill Shanks. 1996. *The New American Voter.* Cambridge, MA: Harvard University Press.

Morin-Chassé, Alexandre, Damien Bol, Laura B. Stephenson, and Simon Labbé St-Vincent. 2017. "How to Survey about Electoral Turnout? The Efficacy of the Face-Saving Response Items in 19 Different Contexts." *Political Science Research and Methods* 5 (3): 575–84.

Mueller, D. 2003. *Public Choice III.* Cambridge: Cambridge University Press.

Nevitte, Neil, André Blais, Elisabeth Gidengil, and Richard Nadeau. 2009. "Socio-Economic Status and Non-Voting." In *The Comparative Study of*

Electoral Systems, ed. H.D. Klingemann, 85–108. Oxford: Oxford University Press.

Niemi, Richard G., and M. Kent Jennings. 1991. "Issues and Inheritance in the Formation of Party Identification." *American Journal of Political Science* 35 (4): 970–88.

Nyhan, Brendan, Christopher Skovron, and Rocio Titiunik. 2017. "A Differential Registration Bias in Voter File Data." *American Journal of Political Science* 61 (3): 744–60.

Ojeda, Christopher, and Julianna Pacheco. 2019. "Health and Voting in Young Adulthood." *British Journal of Political Science* 49 (3): 1163–86.

Owen, Guillermo, and Bernard Grofman. 1984. "To Vote or Not to Vote: The Paradox of Nonvoting." *Public Choice* 42 (3): 311–25.

Persson, Mikael. 2014. "Testing the Relationship between Education and Political Participation Using the 1970 British Cohort Study." *Political Behavior* 36: 1–21.

Pettigrew, Stephen. 2017. "The Race Gap in Precinct Wait Times: Why Minority Precincts Are Underserved by Local Election Officials." *Political Science Quarterly* 132 (3): 527–47.

Plutzer, Eric. 2002. "Becoming a Habitual Voter: Inertia, Resources and Growth in Young Adulthood." *American Political Science Review* 96: 41–56.

Powell, G. Bingham Jr. 1982. *Contemporary Democracies: Participation, Stability, and Violence.* Cambridge, MA: Harvard University Press.

Prior, Markus. 2010. "You've Either Got It or You Don't? The Stability of Political Interest Over the Life Cycle." *Journal of Politics* 72 (3): 747–66.

–. 2019. *Hooked: How Political Interest Fuels Our Democracy.* New York: Cambridge University Press.

Reuter, Ora John. 2019. "Civic Duty and Voting under Autocracy." Mimeo: University of Wisconsin-Milwaukee.

Riker, William H., and Peter C. Ordeshook. 1968. "A Theory of the Calculus of Voting." *American Political Science Review* 62 (1): 25–42.

Rogers, Todd, and Masahiko Aida. 2014. "Vote Self-Prediction Hardly Predicts Who Will Vote, and Is (Misleadingly) Unbiased." *American Politics Research* 42 (3): 503–28.

Rosenstone, Steven J., and John Mark Hansen. 1993. *Mobilization, Participation and Democracy in America.* New York: Macmillan.

Saris, Willem E., Melanie Revilla, Jon A. Krosnick, Eric M. Shaeffer. 2010. "Comparing Questions with Agree/Disagree Response Options to Questions with Item-Specific Response Options." *Survey Research Methods* 4 (1): 61–79.

Schuman, Howard, and Stanley Presser. 1981. *Questions and Answers in Attitude Surveys: Experiments on Questions Form, Wording, and Context.* New York: Academic Press.

Selb, Peter, and Simon Munzert. 2013. "Voter Overrepresentation, Vote Misreporting, and Turnout Bias in Postelection Surveys." *Electoral Studies* 32 (1): 186–96.

Sinclair, Betsy, Margaret McConnell, and Donald P. Green. 2012. "Detecting Spillover Effects: Design and Analysis of Multilevel Experiments." *American Journal of Political Science* 56 (4): 1055–69.

Singh, Shane P. 2019. "Compulsory Voting and Parties' Vote-Seeking Strategies." *American Journal of Political Science* 63 (1): 37–52.

Stein, Robert M., et al. 2019. "Waiting to Vote in the 2016 Presidential Election: Evidence from a Multi-County Study." *Political Research Quarterly.* Available at https://doi.org/10.1177/1065912919839155.

Stephenson, Laura, André Blais, Damien Bol, and Filip Kostelka. 2017. "Making Electoral Democracy Work." Harvard Dataverse, V2. Available at https://doi.org/10.7910/DVN/RR0NNQ.

Stewart III, Charles. 2012. "Waiting to Vote in 2012." *Journal of Law and Politics* 28: 439–63.

Stockemer, Daniel. 2017. "What Affects Voter Turnout? A Review Article/ Meta-Analysis of Aggregate Research." *Government and Opposition* 52 (4): 698–722.

Sund, Reijo, et al. 2017. "How Voter Turnout Varies between Different Chronic Conditions? A Population-Based Register Study." *Journal of Epidemiology and Community Health* 71: 475–79.

Turgeon, Mathieu, and André Blais. 2019. "Am I Obliged to Vote? Compulsory Voting under Ill-informed Voters." Mimeo: University of Western Ontario, London.

Verba, Sidney, Kay Lehman Schlozman, and Henry E. Brady. 1995. *Voice and Equality: Civic Voluntarism in American Politics.* Cambridge, MA: Harvard University Press.

Wass, Hanna. 2007. "The Effects of Age, Generation and Period on Turnout in Finland 1975–2003." *Electoral Studies* 26 (3): 648–59.

–. 2008. "Generations and Turnout: Generational Effect in Electoral Participation in Finland." *Acta Politica* 35.

Wolfinger, Raymond E., and Steven J. Rosenstone. 1980. *Who Votes?* New Haven, CT: Yale University Press.

Index

Note: Page numbers with (f) refer to figures and (t) to tables.